STARGAZER

PREDICTIONS
FOR 2005
—and beyond!

PUBLISHER'S NOTE

Anthony Carr's predictions for 2005 were made
and completed by June 30, 2004.

This included George W. Bush's re-election,
Yassar Arafat's death, and that Osama bin Laden was not
dead and would threaten the world once again.

I hope you enjoy this book and thank you for purchasing it.

Bill Hushion, *Publisher*
November, 20, 2004

STARGAZER

PREDICTIONS FOR 2005
—and beyond!

A Question of Fate.
Was God a Star Traveller?
Plus: Hands of Destiny.

ANTHONY CARR

"The World's _Most Documented_ Psychic!"

Hushion House
PUBLISHING

*This book is dedicated
to my mother,
Josephine Heughan
(nee Lonsdale)*

ISBN 0-9733212-6-1

Carr, Anthony
STARGAZER
Predictions For 2005 *and Beyond!*
Divination/Predictions

Published by
Hushion House Publishing
36 Northline Road
Toronto, Ontario, Canada M4B 3E2
Printed and Bound in Canada

Cover and interior design by Fortunato Design Inc.

ACKNOWLEDGEMENTS

My thanks go out to the following people for their excellent contributions to my book, and to my life.

Allen Spraggett (Doctor of Divinity, former religion editor of the Toronto Star, author of fourteen books on the paranormal). A genius whose knowledge is truly encyclopedic, a living, walking university who has passed on his erudition to me (as much of it as I could absorb) and possesses the patience of Job, in forever buffeting the tidal wave of Sisyphean questions about "the meaning of life." (Not to mention his being responsible for my very first television appearance.) For all this, I am deeply grateful.

Les Pyette (emeritus CEO, Toronto Sun Publishing Corporation) without whose "nose for news" and special "Insight" most of my projects never would have seen the light of day. This puts him head and shoulders above the rest, for which I shall always be indebted.

To the memories of CFRB's legendary **Gordon SinClair** (author of "The Americans") who introduced me to radio, late Toronto Sun columnists **Paul "The Rimmer" Rimstead**, **George Cunningham-Tee** and dear **Dave Bailey** for their encouragement, support and mentorship; not to mention **Glen Woodcock** (still on the Earth Plane) for opening the door.

The talented **Ray Parrish** for his wonderful illustrations and editorial input.

Carola Vyhnak (Toronto Star) for having the guts to publish many of my outrageous and startling predictions beforehand—namely 9/11!

B.J. DelConte (former UPI Bureau Chief, now City-TV talk-show host) for his years of support.

Richard McIlveen (CFTO-TV News Producer), for allowing me to annually broadcast my New Year predictions—in spite of heavy opposition from his "higher ups."

Former National Enquirer, Examiner and Globe Editor **Joe Mullins**, for introducing my work to the highly entertaining and often controversial world of "the tabloids," lo these many years ago.

Ben E. King (of "Stand By Me" fame) for generously donating his valuable time and name to my projects and world predictions.

Kenise and **Fintan Kilbride**, respectively of Ryerson University (professor of early childhood education) and Neil McNeill High School (English and Latin), for their bulwark toleration of my interminable questions about grammar and prose. Bless you both.

Legendary **"Rompin'" Ronnie Hawkins**, who gave me my first job (as a saxophone player) and has guided me throughout my career with his colorful, cracker-barrel philosophies.

Tina and **Paul Higgins**, **Niall Reid** and **Jonathan Bowness**, for their meticulous research, proof-reading and writing skills, without which this book never would have made the "deadline."

Carlos DaSilva (President, "**Limelight Entertainment**") for under-writing *all* my "ambitions," both financially and emotionally.

And Finally **Jacqueline Stallone** (and family) for all her kindnesses to me, through sickness and health, and for opening the door to the wonderful glittering world of Hollywood, which otherwise would have been impossible.

What people are saying about Anthony Carr

Anthony has read for the crowned heads of Europe and Hollywood, including: **Sylvester Stallone, Richard Burton, Lillian Gish, Liv Ullman, Peggy Lee, James Doohan** ("Beam me up, Scotty!"), **Gorbachev, Phyllis Diller, Queen Juliana** (of The Netherlands), **Lady Iris Mountbatten** (cousin to Queen Elizabeth), **Elke Sommer, Douglas Fairbanks, Jr., Kato Katlin** (O.J.'s houseboy), **"Shock Jock" Howard Stern, Roseanne Barr, Jon Stewart** (*The Daily Show*) and Academy Award winner **Glenda Jackson**, now leader of Britain's Labour Party.

"His track record for predicting major events is well-documented and truly astounding." (**Mark Bonokoski**—Editor, *Ottawa Sun*)

"Dubbed as **'the seer without peer,'** Anthony Carr is the internationally acclaimed psychic-to-the-stars who foresees with chilling accuracy the events that shake and shape our world, and has often been hailed by reputable media persons as **a modern day Nostradamus!**" (**B.J. Del Conte**—Toronto Bureau Chief of United Press International [UPI] News Agency)

From **Tom Snyder**, with regard to one of Anthony's predictions about him on his "LATE, LATE SHOW"—"Mr. Carr ... from your mouth to God's Ear...."

"He is this country's most published and respected psychic and palmist ..." (**Ted Woloshyn**—CFRB, Toronto)

"The more bizarre Anthony's predictions, the more accurately they are fulfilled! I find him quite remarkable...." (ENERGY—108 (Radio) Breakfast Show with **Anwar Knight**)

"What is this—Anthony Carr's Psychic Line? What are you—
a comedian and a Psychic?!" (**Howard Stern**—November 19,
1999)

"You're crazy! How could you know those things about me?
Nobody else does!" (**Roseanne Barr**—December 14, 1999)

Here are some of Anthony's fulfilled predictions from 2004— and previous years.

Attack on America by Arabs! "New York will be devastated by Arabs who wear the red turban and whose emblem is the crescent moon and star," (9/11); Major advances in spinal cord research: "**Dead legs will walk again**"; The murder of **Pope John Paul I** (poisoned!); the death of **Princess Grace**; **The Faulkland Islands War**; the tragic downing of the **Pan Am flight over Lockerbie**, Scotland; the last (1994) "**Killer Quake**" in California; the "**Chunnel**" between England and France; the horrific Mideast overture to Armageddon (**Desert Storm**); the eruption of **Mt. St. Helens**; the **bombing of The Statue of Liberty** and "**The White House Dome**" (Senate Building); the assassination attempt on **Pope Paul John II** and former **U.S President George Bush**; the near death experience of Bloc Quebecois leader **Lucien Bouchard** which claimed his leg; Ex Prime Minister **Brian Mulroney** to become the first former PM in the history of Canada to be accused of corruption and racketeering.

Several Anthony Carr Predictions for 2003 —and Beyond Fulfilled!

San Francisco Bridge—Destroyed!
Statue of Liberty—Destroyed!
"Lady Justice" Superior Court Building—Destroyed!
All destroyed!—But at the Movies!
(FROM "THE CORE," 2003)

And this 2004 prediction: "New York City swamped by a tidal wave! I 'see' flooding in New York! Fires throughout posh

Beverly Hills and surrounding area! Destruction of San Franscico Bridge! Statue of Liberty! Lady Justice Superior Court Buildings! In this sense the world will be hit simultaneously by a double-whammy!"—but again, at the movies, from "THE DAY AFTER TOMORROW" and aren't you glad it is happening only in the movies... (so far)? But, you might remember that, a film is often a precursor to actual world events.

I have developed the unusual ability to not only predict actual world events well in advance, but also coming blockbuster movies and front page newspaper stories; specifically images and photographs. I saw the funerals of Monaco's Princess Grace (Kelly) and that of Princess Diana before they appeared in newspapers worldwide! I saw "E.T., THE EXTRATERRESTRIAL" *in my Mind's Eye* and thought it was an actual coming world event, but it turned out to be a movie. Shortly after, I read the palms of the late, great actor Richard Burton I warned him to take care:

"I see you and a red-headed woman together in a speedboat about to be dashed against jagged rocks!"...at that Burton, glanced up at his manager and asked "Did you show him the script? 'Absolutely not,' " came the reply. Carr had intuited the proposed movie ending.

It seems that most actors live their lives, that is to say, their preferred lives, on stage and film, therefore many of the scenes I have described herein regarding their futures will be reflected in the work they have done and will do in coming roles proposed to them, as opposed to their real terrestrial life, which they along with the rest of us, have come to know and generally despise.

I have long since arrived at the illogical but probably intuitively correct conclusion that the machinations at work in the Cosmos and in our own Psyches are One and the Same Electrical impulse (for want of a better word which does not smack of anthropomorphism or a personal relationship with God or some such stuff), that is utilized in movie making, television broadcasts and also in keeping our hearts beating and synapses synapsing.

My point being that even though I arrived at this following conclusion circuitously, the Cosmos does not seem to differentiate between real events ...and "reel" events. Which leads me to the oft-put question "Well then, what is reality?" After all, if what the Source shows us in our Mind's Eye, which can be from "reel life" or "real life", then whaaat, pray tell, is real?

And what about when we dream? Is that then the true Electrical Us, which is able to wander back and forth across the Universe, throughout Space and Time, unencumbered by our physical bodies? And what if we should die in that moment of sleep? (We should be so lucky!) Would that Divine Spark ("The Soul") simply go on dreaming?... probably.

I saw in my Mind's Eye the image of a terrible tidal wave sweeping across New York City and a gigantic tornado, the biggest I have ever seen—utterly destroy Los Angeles. It seemed so real I was compelled to phone Joe Mullins at The Globe, in Florida, to describe to him my vision. He duly received it (with his perfunctory tongue in cheek attitude), then placed it in his desk drawer of useless "information" and quickly forgot about it. When the movie "THE DAY AFTER TOMORROW" was released in May 2004, here they were, the two disaster predictions—exactly like I had seen them in my Mind's Eye. I called Mullins to remind him of the vision, just as he was preparing to release a spread of that movie's pictures in the Globe—in full color—pictures of the tidal wave and giant tornado destroying New York (Manhattan) and Los Angeles, respectively.

Our Electrical antennae, bye-the-by, comprises the entire neurological system including the pineal gland, which acts as a movie projector and recorder of current, past and future events—*visually*, and cares not whether "said events are from real life or film life. In short, understand that this *is* the application of the laws pertaining to Psychic function. The subtle Electrical, Atomic and Psychic forces of Nature or, if you prefer, our Souls, which are at One and is One with the Universe (though corny as it sounds), not separate.

This is the Eternal Power that simultaneously records in our Psyche all our experiences—forever.

Any war veteran will tell you he carries with him forever *the horrible images and sounds* of what he has experienced in battle, never being able to divest himself of the *terrible memories*, until the day he dies, and perhaps not even then....

Fiction writers such as H.G. Wells and Jules Verne, wrote about future events and inventions a hundred years before they became fact—submarines, planes, helicopters, trips to the moon—although I'm sure at the time they thought their creations were strictly "figments of their imaginations," mere grist for the writer's mill, without any thought that they were plucking from the Universe images of Future Events and machines, much in the manner Hollywood writers and movie producers do today.

In fact, *today*, August 29, 2004, even as I am currently desperately writing to finish off this manuscript before publication deadline, I saw a movie last night—a comedy—called "WITHOUT A PADDLE."

There is a burial scene in which the priest/minister recites the eighteenth (18th) psalm!... In all my years of attending movies (considerable—probably thousands!) and the same number of *real* (not "reel") funerals, I have never, not *ever*, heard anyone—on or off screen—invoke such an obscure psalm except, of course, by me—here and now—in the previous chapter of this book—namely: "Was God a Star Traveller?" by which I use it to suggest that possibly "God" was, and Is, a galactic star-hopper. This is yet another example of "celluloid syncrinicity."

Whatever the Electrical process at work which allows us to mentally "snap photo images" and "hear" (in our minds) the recorded voices, sounds and music of *daily life* and *activity on Earth* is the same element used in motion pictures, radio and television. It is the same Power.

All events—on stage and in actual life—are recorded in the Great Beyond, the Cosmic Camera, Akashsic records or, simply the Universe.

"Whole face transplants and re-plants will become common place throughout the medical and cosmetic industries for people who have been severely disfigured, i.e., faces torn off by machinery or destroyed by fire." (Prophesied in June, "Anthony Carr's Predictions for 2005—and Beyond!), to wit: "Entire face transplants for the severely disfigured through disease, fire or injury—now in experimental stage." (Toronto Star, August, 2004; Canadian Medical Post, August, 2004)

World Events

"It won't be long before president elect George W. Bush plunges the world into war!" and, "The Mid-East will explode like a roman candle, drawing all nations ever closer to WW III!"...

These two chilling prophesies I made in 2001, and now that President Bush has precipitated the overture to Armageddon, we are well on our way to World War III. In one way or another, the 9-11 terrorists must be weeded out. There is no turning back now.

That said, I predict that President **George W. Bush** will be assassinated or impeached, whichever comes first. Ditto for British Prime Minister **Tony Blair**. In the end, America, Canada and the rest of the free world will come out of this magnificently. All that's required is a little courage, calm and determination to fight when necessary and the Will to do so, for the good life always comes at a cost—the cost of sometimes putting one's self in harms way. Persistence and determination alone are Omnipotent and will carry us through to victory in the coming tribulation.

Education will not. Hitler, the tyrant, first destroyed all educators and books. Genius will not... unrewarded genius is almost a proverb—and likewise talent. Guts, persistence and calm in the face of danger *will* solve and always has solved the problems of the world created by despots.

We simply cannot allow a bully to get the upper hand. We just can't! God bless the Canadians, the Americans and the British—and all our allies.... I'm old enough to remember what we were capable of—and proved!—during World War II.

We've just forgotten *how*—and just how tough we *really can be* when push comes to shove! And if don't get tough, we are going to pay an *unparallel penalty* for refusing to see the truth! For burring our heads in the sand. Peace will come, but ultimate peace will not come until the Star-Travelers return. They will establish His throne on Earth!!!

Anthony Carr's most recent predictions and others which are unfolding— even as we speak

"That Palestinian leader Yasser Arafat will die mysteriously...." (Prophesied June, 2004), to wit: "Palestinian leasder Yasser Arafat, dies of mysterious illness!" (November 10, 2004; CNN).

Danger to the President! President Bush to be elected to another term in office but assassinated before its end. (Prophesied in June, "Anthony Carr's Predictions for 2004— and Beyond!)

"It won't be long before President-elect George W. Bush plunges the world into war." (Prophesied January 1st, 2001)

"That Osama bin Laden is most certainly not dead, and will resurface periodically to *verbally* threaten the free world, before he or his corpse is captrured." (Prophesied, Toronto Sun, January, 2003), to wit: "Bin Laden resurfaces with election warning!" (Toronto Globe and Mail, October 30, 2004).

"The Mideast will explode like a roman candle in 2001, drawing all nations ever closer to WW III!" (Prophesied January 2001)

"I see raging fires around the White House in Washington D.C.!!" (Prophesied January 2001)

"Sabotage of the D.C. senate building (white dome)—black smoke and fire!" (Prophesied January 2001)

"A great disaster will strike a major city to create a yawning chasm as earth and buildings topple into eternity." (Prophesied January 2001)

That "wrinkled rocker" **Mick Jagger** will finally receive his much coveted knighthood," (Prophesied, Toronto Sun, June 2002), to wit: "Mick Jagger was finally knighted."

That "great orange fireball with black corona will explode high over Toronto," (Prophesied, Toronto Sun, July 2002), to wit: "A tremendous gas explosion occurred when lightning struck a main gas line, creating a huge burst of fire high over the city."

That "a 'miracle' will manifest at Ground Zero, New York, one last sign for all to unite in world peace *before it's too* late!" (Prophesied, Toronto Sun, February 2002), to wit: "The day on which all the Broadway stars, and citizens from all parts of the world, joined hands together at 'that terrible place' in a defiant show of solidarity."

That "a fatal outbreak of Mad Cow disease will strike Canada and quickly spread across the country and the U.S." (Prophesied, Toronto Sun, August 2002), to wit: "Man dies of variant Creutzfeldt-Jacobs disease (mad cow) in Saskatoon, Saskatchewan, Canada."

That "a fire will break out at the Santa Monica Pier," (Prophesied, Toronto Sun, February 2002), to wit: "Fire breaks out at Santa Monica Pier, arson suspected."

That a "giant comet like 'object'—visible even by day—will appear on the horizon, heralding momentous global changes," (Prophesied, Toronto Sun, August 2002), to wit: "Large meteor to miss earth by mere inches (in space terms) on Saturday, August 17,2002."

That "top-chop king **Steven Segal** will move to music to 'sing' the blues and play the harp," (Prophesied, Toronto Sun, June 2002), to wit: "Action star Steven Segal *'sings the blues'* as mafia extorts millions from the actor for allegedly maneuvering him into several major movie roles, over the years."

That "former U.S. President **Bill Clinton** will host an incredibly successful TV variety talk-show," (Prophesied ,Toronto Sun, June 2002), to wit: "It has been announced that the major American networks are lining up offer former U.S. President *Bill Clinton* a prime time television variety show on which he will be able to 'blow his own horn' (being that he is, *after all*, a saxophone player)."

That "**Al Waxman** will perform one last time on stage, his swan song," (Prophesied, Toronto Sun, May 2002), to wit: "A statue of the late star of 'The King of Kensington' and 'Cagney and Lacey' was unveiled in a blaze of media coverage, in the old Kensington district of Toronto. Hundreds of celebrities attended the ceremony."

That "**Catherine Clark**, daughter of former Canadian Prime Minister **Joe (who?) Clark**, will surprise everyone by announcing her (sudden and unexpected) marriage to a tall, dark handsome young man and will possibly pursue Federal politics," (Prophesied, Toronto Sun, August 2002), to wit: "Catherine Clarke surprised everyone by suddenly marring a politically unknown young man (Chad Schella) last week in a private ceremony. Catherine has also announced her intentions—in the near future—to pursue federal politics."

That "**Pamela Wallen** will survive her colon cancer and enjoy excellent health in a new career in front of the cameras," (Prophesied, Toronto Sun, July 2002) to wit: *"Pamela Wallen* has accepted the prestigious government posting in New York as Canadian Consul General, which she is excitedly looking forward to, now that she successfully won her battle with colorectal cancer."

That "**Princess Margaret** will pass on in 2002," (Prophesied, Toronto Sun, February 2002), to wit: "Princess Margaret Dies!"

That "**Mike Tyson** has one more good fight pay day before he's through," (Prophesied, Toronto Sun, June 2002), to wit: "Tyson K.O.'d by Lennox Lewis!

"A successful bombing of the Staten Island Ferry! New York City will be rocked by multiple disasters; riots, Earthquakes, chemical spills," (Prophesied January 2001 and August 2003), to wit: "10 die in New York Staten Island Ferry Disaster! (Toronto Star, October 16, 2003)."

"I see the Eiffel Tower, or perhaps a similar structure like the CN Tower destroyed … toppled onto its side! This will mark the beginning othe awful and terrible war!" (Prophesied January 2001)

"The Empire State Building explodes from a terrorist bomb! In a futile attempt to demoralize America, Arab terrorists, who wear the red turban and whose emblem is a 'star and crescent moon,' are responsible." (Prophesied January 2001)

"The Mighty Eagle will do battle with the cowardly snake— to victory!!! This I prophesy 100%!!!" (Prophesied January 2001)

"A terrible and certainly unexpected earthquake will hit New York City!" (Prophesied January 2001)

"There will be a terrible plane crash over New York City hundreds are killed." (Prophesied January 2001)

"During 2001, civilization will experience a vigorous return to all things cultural. A Renaissance, like a supernova that burns brightest just before the end." (Prophesied January 2001)

"A horrific 1918 Spanish Flue-like virus will sweep around the world, destroying more human life than did the previous two world wars." (Possibly more Anthrax-like bacteriological weapons!) (Prophesied January 2001)

"Watch for a sign in the heavens that will shock the whole world! It will be like a bolt of lightning or in the form of a UFO—and put the fear of God in us. I feel a great revelation for the world, as if the entire population is coming to its collective senses and we realize we have to do something before it's too late. The 'me' syndrome will be gone. We'll help each other and band together for protection and for the sake of the survival of the human race. Reversal of celestial and terrestrial events and properties will reverse polarities and moralities and return us to old-fashioned values." (Prophesied January 2001)

"Dr. David Ho, discoverer of the AIDS' cocktail, will fortuitously stumbles onto a similar super vaccine that will halt the deadly disease in its tracks!"

Anthony Carr's Predictions for the Year 2005 and Beyond!

As I sit here, pen in hand, attempting to ponder the Imponderable, I have come to accept with calm certainty, as only a person weary of fighting against the inevitable can, that The Skein of Destiny which weaves it's way through all our lives, is as inescapable and unalterable as Life and Death itself. Our Fate, and that of the World, was written in The Sands of Time and in The Stars of Heaven long before we were ever born, and there is not one thing that any one of us can do to change it.

There seems to be prevalent these days a groundswell of uneasiness felt by all the peoples of the world, especially "The Baby Boomers"—the generation born of my era, roughly between 1940 and 1949. A sense of impending doom, that something bad is coming down the pike. This feeling keeps nagging at these war-time babies (—and maybe they're right!). "I was born during a war and I will probably die during a war!" is the often repeated refrain heard these days around the world. This "ill-feeling" has been created by the transiting "bolt out of the blue" planet Uranus, leaving the sign of Aquarius where it sat comfortably for the past seven years. This created a "feel good" period of excitement and adventure because it formed a favorable trine (a 120 degree angle to the natal Uranus in Gemini), which is where it was in the 1940 to 1949 period when this generation was born. (By-the-bye, transiting means where the planet is moving through the Heavens now, *today*, and natal means whatever sign it was going through *on the day you were born*—the instant the Universe snapped a picture of it—a picture attached to you for the duration of this life's experience).

Unfortunately the transiting Uranus of today has recently moved out of Aquarius and into Pisces, thus creating a square, or a 90 degree angle to the natal Uranus in Gemini, which is now causing all this personal uneasiness—not to mention all kinds of unexpected World Chaos and upsets. This is occurring because the delicate Electrical balance of Life in each of us and our Solar System and Universe (and Multi-verse), right down to the cellular level of the amoeba, has been upset (to say the least); so our general "Feeling of Uneasiness" is well founded. But fear not, for this too shall pass...in about seven years.

Get ready for the new phenomenon of "Re-birth charts." You probably know your own birth sign—most people do. What you are not familiar with is who or what you were in a previous existence—that is to say—a previous existence of your Electrical Energy Field—where from your *Future* incarnation may be determined!

When you "gasp your last," that exact moment "you shed this mortal coil," an astrologer can make a Re-birthchart based on the position of the planets in the Heavens the *instant* you pass on, and tell you who or what you will return as the moment you exit, then enter, your new receptacle. If you return as human, you can will your estate to your Future self. If as animal, then leave your goods to the A.S.P.C.A. (American Society for the Prevention of Cruelty to Animals) or the Canadian Humane Society. And if mineral or vegetable, perhaps donate to your favorite botanical or geological society. Yes! I predict Re-birth charts to be in vogue in 2005 and I, Anthony Carr, shall forge the way to bring this new concept to the world!...(Or, maybe not.)

America

Osama bin Laden will be brought to New York where co-conspirators will attempt to rescue him, or his remains.

I see **The John Hancock Tower** in Chicago crumbling to the ground. From sabotage or attrition, I know not.

Unless America takes drastic steps to clean up it's act, there will be a biological or nuclear mishap that will make Chernoble look like a light spring shower.... I see many Americans wearing gas and oxygen masks.

More and more "Christian" religious figure heads will be outed as being the largest consumer group of child porn, not to mention the largest group of child molesters! "That which was most high shall be brought most low." (Revelation)

Air quality becomes a pandemic concern as drastic measures are taken to correct this very serious problem. Again, my "Mind's Eye" sees large populations—worldwide—wearing oxygen masks.

As with gas and oil, giant business conglomerates will figure a way to profit from this disaster. Citizens, forced to wear oxygen tanks on their backs, will be charged per gasp! (Don't laugh, "many a truth has been spoken in jest.")
"And the lion shall lie down with the lamb"—because of the necessity to economize on space.

Canada

Canada will build a powerful army, navy and air force which will be sorely needed and has been ever since the first day that **George W. Bush** was elected to the oval office and sowed the seeds of WW III. (And this I predicted while they were yet still counting votes in Florida!)

Nazi Ontario **Premier Dalton McGuinty** will be assassinated for his two-faced legislation of the repressive health tax laws against the poor people of Ontario, a law so backward that the late **Tommy Douglas**, must be spinning in his grave. Shame on you, Dalton, and may the fleas of a thousand camels nest in your armpits.

As the American economy slips into recession, the Canadian GNP (gross national product) will take off. This leads to the Canadian dollar becoming even more valuable to the Yankees— and the burgeoning "Hollywood North" community here in Toronto, Vancouver and elsewhere in The Great White North.

Newfoundland fishing companies face extreme difficulties when large groups of whales wreak havoc on unsuspecting fishing boats.

Catastrophe on the recently completed **Toronto Sheppard Avenue Line**, due by November 2005. Two trains collide resulting in death and injury.

A powerful Metis leader will rise out of the west and attempt to create a new nation under a new Canadian flag.

Psychic pets become the rage as the Universal thirst for knowledge deepens. Psychic channelers will interact with the psyches of our furry friends to help bring about more harmonious understanding between animal and beast (the *latter* being we!)

A string of connected police assaults on University students (especially women) will occur in the London, Ontario, area. Disturbingly high numbers of police officers will be involved.

After a rabid bat is discovered in Toronto, Ontario, Canada, great swarms of the infected animals will be seen flying throughout the land, silhouetted against the night sky's full moon. Their origin, it will be discovered, was Montreal, Quebec.

Even just the threat of former Ontario Premier **Mike Harris'** return to political leadership will create a chain reaction throughout Canada that will develop into the segregation of east and west from central Canada. (Actually, compared to Premier Dalton McGuinty (Psycho's Norman Bates), former Prime Minister Brian Mulrooney and former Ontario Premier Mike Harris(-ment) look like Little lord Fauntleroy!

Tourists—especially Europeans—will flock to Quebec City to experience the mystery of this quaint, most ancient of Canadian cities... a miracle, a revelation—no less greater than the one commemorated at Lourdes—will be the draw!

Quebec Block Party landslide knocks the liberals flat and reopens the door to separation again.

Edmonton oilers finally get a shot at the Stanley Cup....

Calgary, voted number one Canadian City in a poll last year, will enjoy huge increases in everything from real estate to tourism.

Growing popularity of Klondike Days! And as well, I see money flowing in exponentially !!

David Miller, Toronto's new mayor, will boost tourism and prove to be a very good mayor to be re-elected to another term.

Musical group **The Guess Who** will revive their hit song—"Back to Saskatoon"—bringing back much needed attention to that city.

Saskatchewan, long known for its "Big Blue Skies," will be funded by governments to produce great quantities of wheat and grain to supply Canada and half the U.S with food. Farming space will be protected for decades to come because most of land is being overdeveloped.

The Newfoundland Board of Education to publish a compendium of pithy "Newfie Expressions."

Halifax's Mike Clattenburg, director of the now popular hit series "Trailer Park Boys," will branch out to become a Hollywood heavy-hitter.

Nova Scotia will amalgamate with Prince Edward Island and New Brunswick in the near future to become a force to be reckoned with.

British Columbia's "Golden Hills" are to bring yet more skiers from around the world when *real gold* is discovered in "them thar` hills!!"—attracting record numbers of tourists who bring with them copious amounts of "cold cash," a.k.a. paper gold.

Vancouver will see greater numbers of unsavory people because of drug houses. Supplying addicts brings chaos and disaster to this once quaint and quiet town. A new way to help is implemented.

"Stompin Tom Conners" will retire to beautiful Charlottown, and the new national anthem will become "Bud the Spud"... plus, a new flag designed whose emblem is a spud (potato) against a red background.

Ontario's Power Grids are failing drastically because of privatizing. It could put us in a deep freeze comparable to the disaster in Montreal!

Prime Minister **Paul Martin** will turn like his predecessors—lies, lies and more lies!

Earthquakes and giant storms will wash away most of British Columbia's coastline next year. Yet these disasters will not be the last to hit Canada's coast! They but signal the beginning of the strangest weather that Canadians will ever see.

Some day, Lake Ontario will cover Toronto as far North as the 401 highway!... Some day.

Although a tremendous earthquake will shake the city of Barrie, Ontario, the damage will not be severe; however it will lead to the discovery of multiple fault-lines in the area. Some day Lake Ontario will cover Toronto as far north as the 401 highway!... Some day.

America placing wire taps on Canadian citizens! Unbeknownst to the Canadian government the U.S. is keeping close tabs on Canadians, long suspected of running secret training camps for home-bred terrorists.

Royal Canadian Mounted Police discover why water levels of Canadian lakes are getting lower. Giant hoses placed underground by the U.S. have been sucking up one of our greatest resources while blinding us with offers "to buy" our water.

Stockwell Day, Federal member of Parliament—Christian family man? This will be publicly disproved in a twisted Lolita-type story.

World Events

Osama bin Laden, look at my eyes and know this: I swear by Allah and Almighty God that you will never see Paradise, the soft light of Heaven reserved for your most innocent victims, but only the dark and stormy place at Cosmos' end, where Chaos reigns.

There, shall your Sensorial Self — (your soul, should you possess one), languish in unimaginable agony until even It is finally consumed by the Eternal Fire. For you have come 'round on the Great Wheel of Life full circle and not yet learned your lessons. And you never will. In the history of the world there has never been such a single act of utter cruelty in which so many helpless citizens were purposely murdered! Defenseless men, women and children—all. A *real* man would have attacked the military.

You are no *true* follower of Islam. However, you do bear a strong resemblance to Adolph Hitler who, no doubt, would be in awe of your barbarity, were he living. I'm almost certain you *are* the Fuhrer reincarnate, with your pathological hatred of Jews and Americans. And like Hitler, you are probably a self-loathing, *closet* Jew. So why don't you do the world a favor—and kill *yourself!* You are a mad dog and a coward. And mad dogs *must* be put down, as soon you will be. Death will come swiftly. Your suffering in this life will be brief, but interminable in the next.

Both Bible and Qur'an (Koran) state: "The knower knoweth," and I know the horror that hath no words to describe that which awaits you in the Great Beyond. This is a gift of "vision" bestowed on one who has perhaps repeated the great range of life, *too* often.

I would *like* to believe this "Sense of Kismet" might, in some small way, bring a degree of comfort to the grieving who have lost their loved ones. Yet I know it cannot be…only time may ease the pain, console the inconsolable.

Remember, however, that the Paths to God are many and varied, since not all travel the familiar and worn road. But this I promise: the Fate of Osama bin Laden's Soul is sealed, as I swear the Souls of all our dearly departed are Eternally Sealed in the Great Archives of the Akashic Records of Heaven (into which Edgar Cayce occasionally peered to glimpse the future), or in what the Christian Bible calls "The Book of Life," until the Day of Judgement.

To Jews, Muslims and Christians: When Comes the Great and Glorious One *all* eyes will see *but* One, and *only* One shall rule…. He, Who is the Light of the world…. Star-Traveller or God, only He can stop the carnage. And every religion will be One.

Osama bin Laden, this you well know: "What Is Written In The Mind Of Allah (God) *Will Be* And *Must* Come To Pass." But it will not be what you expect. Should I die before this conflict is over, *in whatever manner*, take this as yet another sign of your ultimate defeat at the hands of the American Allies.

You will *never* win. "IT IS WRITTEN."

(P.S. There will be a *very* violent and fatal denouement to the bin Laden problem on or about February 25, 2005 or 2006.)

"Golden idol" worship has gotten so far out of hand that we have left spirituality behind and now believe in nothing but the almighty buck! All this will evaporate with the coming changes in celestial, terrestrial, morals and mores, as we return to old-fashion values — that is, putting the other guy ahead of our *frenetic* pursuit of wealth. The Great Cosmic Architect will jolt us out of our collective somnambulism. 9/11 was merely a dress rehearsal, the first link in a chain of coming pandemic shocking events to bring us back to Consciousness. And God!

It's bitter irony that the cowardly 9/11 attack on America by so-called "terrorists" (a term too good for such scum) coincided with a number used in emergency calls for help—911! For this reason 9/11 will henceforth leave a bittersweet taste in the mouths of North Americans, and all the free world.

Therefore I predict that sometime between Thanksgiving and "Remembrance Day," November 11 (11-11), 2005 or 2006, there will be yet another sneak attack on the United States by these "*snakes* with arms and legs." The significance being in numerological terms, 11-11, another number to be burned into our collective consciousness for all time.

But it will be the swan song of our enemies. America will retaliate with such force it will cause the evil ones to curse their mothers for giving them birth, so devastating will be their destruction. **This is the beginning of World War III!**

New U.S. conscription policies will be violently protested in America as this overture to World War III, now in it's infancy, escalates.

I see mass rioting in Iraq after American troops kill an eight-year old civilian. The child attacks a U.S. military patrol with a hand gun and has to be shot dead. This spreads rage throughout the country.

Then **Osama bin Laden** will surely be brought to justice. *He lives as I write this,* but either he or his corpse will be captured and put on display for all to see that he is after all only a man, and barely that. (Prophesied in June, "Anthony Carr's Predictions for 2004—and Beyond!)

In numerology 11-11, has a powerful cosmological significance. On that day the windows of Heaven shall open wide and the G̲reat O̲ne shall descend to save the lost souls of Earth. All will look up in terror, but need not fear, save the guilty. Violence will end. Peace will reign, all over the world.

But first the most tumultuous days in the *history of the planet* are before us. Remember these numbers: eleven-eleven (11-11).

"THE HEART OF MAN IS DECEITFUL ABOVE ALL THINGS, AND DESPERATELY WICKED!"
(from the BOOK OF JEREMIAH)

God Bless the Innocent

* * *

Iraqi dissidents, unilaterally chosen to replace ousted **Saddam Hussein**, will be currently biding their time for the right moment to turn Iraq into a kind of a superpower, the closest the Middle-East has ever come to such an experience.

A network of pseudo-Muslims attack and leave the next World Youth Day in Cologne obliterated. As a result, the spread of Christianity temporarily falters as people become disillusioned ... not to mention terrified!

British Prime Minister **Tony Blair** reveals he is a closet homosexual ("closet" that is, until now) and has been living with his boyfriend in a London flat for over two years. **Cherie Blair** declares relief at the revelation and says "she's so glad he will have someone to care for him," after which declaration she'll give him the kids and then move ahead to focus on her law career. Eventually he will marry into the royal family.

The discreet birth of an illegitimate child in a private hospital will make headlines around the world. The baby will be birthed by teenage pop-sensation **Brittany Spears** and the father, none other than **Prince Charles**. Although Charles will deny being the father of the child (naturally), he will refuse to take a paternity test, much to the surprise of the public.

Prince Charles, Heir apparent to the British throne, shall grieve for the loss of a child.

Attack on Paris, France, that will render its Eiffel Tower useless. Toppled! (* This was Predicted in 2002 and -3; fire struck July 23, 2003. This is only the beginning of what's to come.)

Locust swarms further cripple Israel's tourism market, damaged already by increased terrorist attacks.

Largest scam in history: gold companies fabricate huge deposits of the yellow stuff in hopes of increasing the value of floundering stocks.

The Biblical Noah's Ark is finally discovered on Mt. Ararat and authenticated once and for all.

Great Buffalo herds will again roam the plains of western America—eventually requiring culling. Buffalo meat replaces beef as an American staple, likewise Canada—followed by the rest of the world.

A Moslem woman will give birth to a Super-Child of the World who will possess supernatural and mystical powers.

A revelation that late American President **Lyndon B. Johnson** was involved in the Assassination of **John F. Kennedy**.

"Gay governor **Arnold Schwarzenegger**,"—screams a headline in a California newspaper! Tongues wag world-wide.

Benny beware! TV evangelist **Benny Hinn** suffers fatal shot to the chest (—perhaps a heart attack?) during a rally.

Coal and peat moss come back—big time—as major fuel sources for industry.

Celebrity deaths: Sadly, **Mohammad Ali** will pass on in 2005, as well as former presidents **Jimmy Carter** and **Gerald Ford**; ditto for former British Prime Minister the **"Iron Lady" Margaret Thatcher**, **Jack "The Odd Couple" Klugman**, jazz pianist great **Oscar Peterson** and thespian **Sydney Poitier**. Accolades for Anne Bancroft before she passes. And Laurn Bacall.

Tremendous destruction at New York Airport! (JFK? LaGuardia?) A terrible blast, much loss of life, on or around October 10/ 2005. Also, simultaneous attacks will occur on other airports in major American and Canadian cities.

A glut of books on WWII and its heroes will flood the global market. This ensures posterity will never forget the high cost of freedom.

Remember this, if you remember nothing else: the number 11/11 will be profoundly important to the survival of the people of the world.

Both the new Toronto hydrofoil (The Breeze) and Titanic II are destined for disaster—especially the Titanic, for to tempt mistress Fate surely is to court one's own demise.

In October or November 2004 or 2005, the world surely shall tremble in fear; then again, in the sign of Taurus (May), there will be a water disaster of titanic proportions.

The new pontiff shall be **Peter of Rome**—who will flee the violent Turk!

Though since long-deceased, this duke and duchess of the world, a brand new scandal sings, and sets all Britain a-whirl.

Helium houses floating above earthquake zones are the coming thing in Southern California; then in other earthquake-weary countries.

American people will come to believe Bush is an exterrestrial alien in human form trying to control the minds of the people. He shall be called Satanail, and comes from the nether reaches of outer space.

A decadent and greedy people will lead a nation into spiritual impoverishment, because a people without belief is nothing and the *pursuit* of material wealth can only end in despair. (Unless of course, you attain it!) North America take heed!

Elderly people become more depressed as the old fundamental belief systems such as Heaven and Hell fall away. This will end when their hopes are renewed by a belief in the return of the **Star-Travellers** and despair is replaced with the certainty of a "life hereafter" in the Electrical Cosmos, to which the Divine Spark returns. In other words, we are going home.

The great tidal wave seen sweeping over Manhattan in the film "THE DAY AFTER TOMORROW" would be as a teardrop in a glass of water, should this planet ever "flip its lid" (that means it's polarities). This happens every 25,000 years, or so.... and is now way overdue!

Once U.S. forces withdraw from Iraq, leaving it vulnerable with only a skeleton army for protection, Iran will attack with such force as to leave the much besieged country reeling and confused. Again America and the coalition get involved. This time, there is no stopping the juggernaut of world intervention....Woe unto us!

The Great Dragon will awaken after its long sleep, to cross the Yangtze and cast its fiery breath upon the world. The Yellow Horde shall rule for five- and twenty years.

Then the Great Dragon will make a pact with the people of the emblem of the "Star and Crescent Moon." Together they will plunge the world into Armageddon!

Pakistan and India—again at each other's throats! America—again forced to intervene. And chaos—again out of control! Is there such a thing as "Controlled chaos"?)

But the Yellow dragon will perch the line to threaten in support of this dispute. Then will the Mighty Eagle swoop down and destroy the Dragon.

Gasoline gougers continue their greedy stranglehold on hapless car owners. The discovery (now on our doorstep) of a new—yet old—power source is revealed, rediscovered from aeons ago, even beyond The Great Flood!

British prime minister **Tony Blair** to be ousted violently—in the manner of Mussolini!

Over the next two years, Gold, Silver and Platinum skyrocket!

Sidney, daughter of **O.J.Simpson**, blows the whistle on her father for the alleged murder of her mother, Nicole Brown Simpson and freind Ronald Goldman (against the advice of her "shrink" who says to put the incident behind her). She wants revenge on behalf of her mother because The Juice "took up with another woman and so was unfaithful."

Countless great sinkholes simultaneously occur throughout Florida causing widespread catastrophe, loss of life and damage ranging in the billions of dollars.

Because women are now independent, men will not be ready for relationships and marriage until their late thirties and even forties—hence a drop in procreation. However, during and after WWIII women will again hide behind their skirts while men go off to fight and die. Once again men will be men and women, women.

Problems arising out of concerns surrounding homosexuality will be no more. A blasé attitude, due in large part to the massive revenues they'll generate world-wide. This perfectly natural third sex will assume powertful leadership positions through their wealth, as they did in days of yore, specifically the peak period of ancient Greece.

Greek culture, art and philosophy will once again rise to world prominence as a result of their general aggressive behavior and ambition. A powerful leader, such as has not been seen since "the days of the ancients," will rise up to take control! With Alexander's ferocity and **Aristotle**'s wisdom he shall lead the courageous but scattered Greeks into a beautiful new era.

Former Iraqi dictator **Saddam Hussein** will lead a revolution in Iraq after he is given back to the Iraqi government by the United States. He shall be freed from prison by rebels, like Napoleon escaping Elba.

Iran, claiming they are harboring none other than **Osama Bin Laden**, will use him as a bargaining chip to negotiate with America.

At the 2008 Summer Olympics there will be a terrorist threat —and worse! Take care to beef up security ten-fold. Ditto for the 2006 Winter Olympics, when mass riots break out after an attack creates widespread panic!

A new oil shortage turns the UN into a pack of snarling dogs as they fight over the allocation of emergency supplies.

Ten years after the fact, **O.J. Simpson** (of murder fame) will find his wife's killer... "through the looking glass darkly."

West Nile virus will run rampant through America and Canadian cities, much to the delight of Arab extremists who hail it as evidence of Allah's Providence and Will.

An accident at sea involving a People's Republic of China sub-marine and a United States aircraft carrier creates tension between the two superpowers, bringing ever closer the threat of open war!

A new group of North American terrorists pull off attacks on nearly every major nuclear power plant across the globe on New Year's Eve, 2006.

The change in European air prices creates a huge panic in North American companies, making stock in Euro lines soar.

After being promoted and publicized by Arab terrorism, medieval punishments such as beheading, hanging and "draw-ing and quartering" will become popular again. For the torture, rape and mutilation of children and animals, it is appropriate.

I see a tall, light-gray brick office building—not unlike the Empire State or The Chrysler buildings—but not necessarily so, toppling to the ground...don't know whether New York? Chicago? Toronto?... Maybe earthquake, maybe terrorists. Great loss of life and property....

Blah-blah-blah—the religions of today will eventually go the way of the dinosaurs. Our literature to be revered as priceless art in much the same way that rare documents—such as The Declaration of Independence—is regarded today.

Canada to be submersed in squalls and tornados like those of the U.S. Mid-West. This unpredictable weather will be such a threat to crops that "Bio-farming" becomes the wave of the future.

Tidal waves seen only in movies become reality! Monstrous circles of water to engulf heavily populated cities will become the "norm" as the Earth's polarities shift! Los Angeles is swal-lowed up in one great gulp of an earthquake—The BIG ONE!! Nevada, Arizona, become new coastlines.

Another Communist submarine disaster (Red Star) some-where in the polar regions—perhaps The Bering Sea. Many nations move quickly to save lives and averts catastrophe! I see fins of whales, porpoises and dolphins—that ilk, of which will be a sign.

An underground transit system is suddenly stricken with chemical compounds.... People sick and dying! This catastrophe can be compared to 9/11! Terrorist group responsible is be flushed out and killed in a violent fire-fight. (Is there any other kind?)

A strange "mutant" bug appears on the horizon due to never ending excavation projects. The world's most brilliant scientists are puzzled! The new strain—although not fatal—sickens hundreds of thousands.

Food becomes a huge entertainment draw! In Los Angeles, Las Vegas, Toronto and New York because today's "good old home cookin' " will be just a memory. People will yearn for the warm security of the comfort foods we all once knew and loved, as children.

Air quality to become so oppresively bad that heat during summer months drives affluent people to seek summer homes in the Arctic Circle!

Electricity becomes precious—even priceless—and the most valuable commodity on the stock Exchange—surpassing even gold and platinum!

A horrible error in science debunks the anti-depressant medication trend. More and more people suddenly experience fatal effects when drug mixes with certain common foods. Lawsuits deluge governments as people finally fight back.

Nicorette Company will be accused of adding hidden ingredient that causes would-be quitters to become *more* addicted to the gum then they were to the cigarettes! Ya' just can't win!

Unless drastic steps are taken, the large quantities of toxins disposed of in our lakes and oceans will pose such a health hazard from dead and dying marine life, that the stench and visible pollution will keep beaches—world wide—abandoned for decades!

Inner strength in men is the virtue for which women will be searching, in the time of tribulation ahead.

Courtney Cox fights losing battle to overcome eating fetish. Her twisted love for food exceeds her desire to be thin and this destroys her career.

Saddam Hussein's remaining followers smuggle thermo-nuclear weapons through Palestine to use at their leader's trial, in an attempt to send Saddam to Allah in blaze of glory. It fails.... Still, a woman will bring about his eventual ultimate demise. (As I keep predicting.)

America will attack Iran on or about October 11, 2005.

Leftist rebels in Columbia attempt to assassinate U.S. President **George W. Bush** for his support of the Colombian government.

Keep your flashlights handy, a blackout hits North America again!—wiping out the continent's entire power supply. Martial law is declared and military forces are rushed in to halt rioting and looting.

Nuclear explosions in South Korea put surrounding countries at risk from fallout. However rather than explain the explosions, they in fact deny the whole incident!

Saudi Arabia suddenly turns from America. Soldiers stationed there are taken prisoner and publicly tortured. America puts Saudi Arabia on its list of terrorist countries and prepares for war!

America will completely militarize Israel and defend her against the Palestinians—indeed against all on-comers.

U.S. will infiltrate the Palestinian security apparatus....**Arafat** mysteriously dies.

Spain attacks Morocco, setting off a new wave of colonialism in North Africa.

Neo-Nazi and right-wing extremists stage the biggest rally ever at Nuremburg.

Germany will declare a Fourth Reich and elect a portly man from Bavaria as its Fuhrer, for nostalgic reasons.

China sneak attacks Taiwan to wrest political control from the Taiwanese. America looks the other way, citing substantial trade with China.

This Pope dies before year's end or very early in the new one. The conclave to elect an ultra-right Pope, who calls for a new

Christian Crusade against Moslem extremists.

AIDS continues its spread across Africa, killing tens of thousands and destroying whatever is left of the social infrastructure.

Fidel Castro falls gravely ill and dies from poisoned tobacco. Many mourn his loss, including former President **Jimmy Carter**, **Meryl Streep** and **Jesse Helms**, who has a spiritual conversion during the deathbed vigil.

Docu-king **Michael Moore** in grave danger of succumbing to a fatal disease which appears "quite natural" ...perhaps Bush-itis.

Over the sea, with tremendous speed, shall come a man holy in nature, but not by Earthly context, to right the wrongs of Past, Present and Future.

The dawn of the "New Dons" is just around the corner (a New York Corner). These new men of "respect" will be more bloodthirsty than any that preceeded them.

Discovery of a new kind of antibiotic greatly changes the complexion of medicine. For cancer patients—new hope! This "miracle drug" is a giant step towards the eradication of the deadly disease.

With the completion of HMS TRITON, the pride of England, Britannica rules the waves once again.

A meteor from deep space enters Earth's atmosphere over the Sahara Desert with the crack of a thousand thunders. The giant space rock—composed of unidentifiable properties—rains down on the desert turning an arid land into a lush oasis.

Documents time-sealed in the vaults of the CIA will be released to the public by a slightly insane bookeeper, shocking the world when it is discovered that not only did **Bush Jr.** know beforehand about 9/11, but was complicit by not taking immediate action to prevent the disaster.

Osama bin Laden's hiding place to be discovered! Uncovered not by his appearance but by fingerprints left on a glass. His features will have been altered by orders from very, very prominent members of the U.S. government and others residing in America who were in on the 9/11 attacks.

A second moon appears in the heavens! This compounds the power of the unbelievable size of the tidal waves that'll turn once land-locked nations into islands!

New York faces rebellion! The denizens who reside in the bowels of The Big Apple will ascend en masse to overrun the hated surface dwellers!

Space aliens abduct astrophysicists and replace them with their own, in order to prevent Earthlings from successfully making intergalactic journeys!

Great Russia, continuing in its age-old quest for the warm waters of the Mediterranean sea, shall wage war against their neighbors to the south (Turkey) in hopes of conquering the great city/seaport of Istanbul (Constantinople)!

The Israeli Wall will stand, despite the International Court ruling in The Hague that "the wall gravely infringes on the rights of the Palestinians." The wall will effectively result in dividing the world as this new Iron Curtain plunges us back into the darkness of another cold war.

A covert underground war will rage between field officers of the CIA and the Canadian Equivalent, CSIS. What makes this event the more surprising is that CSIS is hired by The American Conservatives charged with the task of digging up as much dirt as possible to use against Bush, Jr. and his administration.

A tragic accident takes place on the Jordan River! A boat laden with Jewish children strikes a large, submerged object and the craft explodes!—a tremendous fireball seen for miles. Everyone will believe it was an act of terrorism! Discovered too late, this act of Fate lets loose "the dogs of war!"

I "see" in America a great concrete dam bursting forth great flood waters throughout the arid land! (Hoover Dam? Boulder Dam?)

Medicine

A solution will be discovered that will stick to the plaque-like substance that causes Alzheimer's. It stops but a moment to photograph it (the substance) then leaves before causing damage to the patient.

Believe it or not! Men will give birth!

From the Cosmos comes an Electrical cure-all for the litany of neurological diseases—including MS (Multiple Scerosis), MD (Muscular Dystrophy) and ALS (Lou Gherig's Disease).

World-wide cessation of rain forest destruction! With the sudden realization of the magnitude of ozone layer damage—and the plethora of possible *new cures* for the multitude of diseases that plague mankind, which would cease with their demise.

Efforts to find a cure for cancer are temporarily halted by the discovery of a new and almost undetectable strain of this already deadly disease. But miraculously, out of this strain comes the genetic secret for *all* its variant causes and cures!

Hectic living has everyone seeking new remedies to keep up with life's pressures. A miracle pill to soon be available that'll have everyone rushing to doctors for this fabulous drug which provides greater energy to be more productive.

Alarming news about the plastic surgery industry! Reality shows like Fox's "The Swan," which follows average looking women through their "surgical quests for beauty," heavily influence weak-minded viewers to seek unneccesary surgery. Countless people die on operating tables! Surgeons are fined for performing dangerous procedures without explaining risks—all for money!!!

Teen drug-use will escalate as they continue to emulate a lifestyle set by the media which is not based on fact. Slow down! Take a reality check!

Global warming will take a tragic toll on lives as air thickens into a black, soupy smog, that lies heavy on our shoulders.

Wealthy people will be able to buy planets *beyond* our own

solar system!... the poor, however, will remain on Earth as it becomes a dying planet. New life *shall flourish* in our own solar system... "...and the *meek* (which rhymes with *weak*) *shall inherit the Earth*."

A super nutrition pill will be invented to offset nourishment-loss from conventional sources. (Like the U-25 pill that "Mighty Mouse" used to take.)

With delusional and idealistic Neptune transiting Aquarius, left wing Shangri-la "love and let love" views will generate a sense of "well-being" (much like alcohol does) over the next seven years or so, to offset the negativity of the Baby Boomer generation created by Uranus going through Pisces.

A new spread of Creutzfeldt-Jakob disease—commonly known as "Mad Cow Disease"—will develop a natural immunity *itself* which medicine will take and modify for a vaccine, strange though that sounds.

Entertainment

Coming on the heels of screenwriter **Joe** ("Show Girls") **Eszterhas**'s repentance, Hollywood will place a ban on smoking in movies. The move to be applauded by bleeding heart liberals and attacked by civil liberties unions. (So, what else is new?)

Something snaps inside **Martha Stewart**, and she slowly begins to develop acute paranoid schizophrenia because of the negative publicity. She'll spend at least three months in an institutition... mental, that is.

Movies and television will move toward scripts with positive themes that have a good influence on weak-minded people who identify too much with characters in film. The public will not be able to blame Hollywood dream-makers for violent acts committed by morons.

TV diva **Oprah Winfrey** to be honored at the Kennedy Center for The Performing Arts—and may even, perhaps, one day win The Nobel Peace Prize.

Because of over-saturation, only superstars will emerge successfully from the avenue of Reality TV.

Jessica Simpson will ostensibly become the next Sandra Dee, with her much publicized life, marriage and extended family out there for all to see. But as the new representative of the "girl next door" image she will rise above her problems, unlike Sandra Dee.

As little **Tommy Cruise**'s career slowly sinks in the West, especially after his last two movie bombs, he'll start sucking up to **Nicole Kidman** to win her back so he can ride her coat-tails, because her career *will continue* to skyrocket!

Teen sensation **Hillary Duff** takes the world by storm outdoing even **Avril Lavigne** and **Britney Spears** but, like many young celebrities who can't handle success ("too much, too soon") she'll begin to slide into the dark, seedy underworld of drugs, booze and "gangstas"—finding this element infinitely more interesting and exciting than mere showbiz.

During a routine broadcast of a popular Reality Show—a death occurs!... Witnessed by millions, the incident results in a cause celebre plunging it and the other shows of its ilk into a tailspin. Of course, this will only serve to incite the blood lust of the populace who'll be screaming for more! Shows that survive the brutal cut will be strictly monitored and subjected to rigorous safety regulations. (I believe the death will occur on the new "Reality Boxing" show hosted by **Sylvester "Rocky" Stallone**.)

Michael Moore, director of such controversial films as "Bowling for Columbine," is in danger of assassination by the United States Government, a retaliatory act for releasing his latest documentary "Fahrenheit 9/11" which is highly critical of President Bush's Sept.11 actions (or non-actions). Michaels's best insurance against death is to broadcast to the world, "Should anything happen to me, even if I'm struck by lightning in bed, it'll be Bush's doing."

David and **Courtney Cox-Arquette**'s showbiz daughter, **Coco**, will contract showbiz fever when **Shirley Temple** movies are re-done, with Coco playing the lead.

Thanks to the sensational "Shrek" movies, the Cinderella-syndrome will finally be debunked forever, much to the glee of teens the world over making for happier, healthier young people.

MC Hammer, currently starring on MTV's The Surreal Life, will return to the music industry taking his earnings from television to record a new album that soars to the top of the charts. But Hammer's "re-fame" will be short-lived after he's caught in a compromising position with co-star **Gary Coleman**.

The Beastie Boys' (Mike D.,MCA, Adrock) views on Tibetan freedom will change drastically when they are injured by guerilla fighters on a good-will trip to Tibet.

Brad Pitt and **Jennifer Aniston** become "yesterday's news" as a couple—and leads to a very public divorce! The split results in Brad's rising up, like the Phoenix from its ashes, to reclaim his "Hollywood status" after the fiasco of being completely miscast in Troy.(Casting director must have been a descendent of **Hellen Keller**, rather than **Helen of Troy**!)

Ben Affleck will lose out as a Hollywood hunk when he balloons up to 300 pounds.

Matt Damon will be "outed" (much to his dismay) and this, of course, costs him juicy straight roles—leaving nothing but feminine charactor parts (like "As Good as It Gets" star, Roy Kinnear). The upshot is—he's straight!

Mike Meyers to remain loyal Canadian. He's learned that loyalty to his country is greatly admired, unlike his Canadian comic counterpart, **Jim Carey**.

Shania Twain becomes Canada's new songbird, knocking the pins out from under beloved *snowbird* of yesteryear, Anne Murray, whose name in Native Canadian (and native American, for that matter)—is "squawking crow."

Brian Adams trades his guitar for a paint brush, which brings him even greater success! Although he's best known for his Canadian music, his popularity will skyrocket in the art circles of New York!

Polo becomes the new trend for the next Hollywood "In Crowd," leaving poker in second place. However, due to their lack of experience there is no end to the broken bones, which they proudly display as a "rite of passage."

Will Farrell, another alumnus of Saturday Night Live, to become a superstar and emulating the likes of other former grads such as Mike Myers, **Dan Akroyd** and **Eddie Murphy**. With one hit already tucked neatly under his belt he'll be offered a role that sends his career through the stratosphere—and make him the highest paid male actor in Hollywood.

Cher finds herself doing farewell concerts well into her 70s (unlike Streisand), because she'll never leave the glitz and glamour of showbiz. You'll never see *her* planting gardens and doing charity work. In fact, the *older* she gets the more attractive to the gay world she'll become—ergo, the more live concerts she'll be in demand to do.

Robert Downey, Jr., finally learns his lesson—alas, too late! He'll have wasted so much time rehabilitating himself that Hollywood will tire of him—even though his antics were far more entertaining than his movies. Temporarily slipping into obscurity, as did **David Curuso** and **John Travolta** (or "Relvolta," as some prefer), his only hope is that he'll be humble enough to beg for a television series—which he'd get!

Ex Prez **Bill Clinton**'s book brings him new found stardom when it's translated into a made-for-T.V. blockbuster movie, much to the dismay of wife, Senator Hillary Clinton. Exposing old wounds, this will incite her to outdo him with yet another book of her own, telling her side—*truthfully*—and embarrassing her hubby straight to the divorce courts.

"Cape Fear"'s **Julliette Lewis** will become famous as a musician-singer. Her lackluster career is waffling, so it's time to emerge once again as the talented star she truly is, albeit in a new arena, instead of the dozy, sleazy "trailer-trash" strumpet roles she continually plays (—and of which, I am certain, she is sick to death!)

CSI, the phenomenal hit series, will try to expand the show to the dismay of original cast members. **William Peterson** (an original) will pull out of his contract leaving the other cast members to scurry about for work in the New York production. Only a few will survive the transition, such as **Marge Helgenberg**.

British television becomes the new thing to watch! Young people and elite groups will surge forth as the next British invasion. (Remember the **Beatles**?) Only people in cliquey circles will manage to mingle and mix with the new English Superstars.

Hollywood stars to flex muscles... brains, not buttocks! **Jodie Foster** has a Harvard degree, **James Woods** and **Gena Davis** are both Mensa members—to mention a few! The coming trend of Hollywood success will be determined by intelligence, leaving dum-dums out in the cold.

Michael Jackson will mirror O. J. Simpson—ending his career.... Money depleted, spent on payoffs and lawyers, Michael has danced his last waltz and it will take more than a moon-dance to keep him grounded.

Jack Nicholson, once the most sought after star in the world, may find himself panning for gold in "them thar' Hollywood Hills" for a living...(Or maybe it's just an "illusion of a scene" from one of his upcoming movies.)

Mattie Staepanek... the brave little poet has passed on his spirit of harmony so that others may benefit from this child's bravery. He has touched the heart of everyone and carried in his frail little hand, "the flame" of a cure for Muscular Dystrophy.

Kim Bassinger and **Alec Baldwin** finally consent to an "out of court" co-sharing of their daughter, Ireland, who is the one suffering from all the jousting. Alec will reluctantly allow his daughter—whom he dearly loves—to go live with her mother, since this is what the child desperatly wants, thus debunking his rep as a Hollywood bully.

Oprah Winfrey becomes a huge—HUGE! player in Hollywood, tipping the scales at 300 pounds! After her network TV contract ends, she'll work behind the scenes to help produce progressive TV talk-shows such as Dr. Phil or even spin-offs of self- help hits, that'll bring her still more fame and fortune. A Nobel prize or an award from the Kennedy Center for the Performing Arts is definitely in her future. I "*see*" it!

Charleze Theron will scrambling for decent roles—thinking she may never top her "MONSTER" Oscar-winning performance. After spending a few years onstage and in television, searching for that "perfect part," once again—tragedy strikes! And once again she survives, trumps her nemesis by utilizing the experience to win even greater acclaim! But I see more blood and violence around her!—And yes, it could be just a movie about her early life, However I believe this is a *two-part* vision that *must* come to pass!

Ex-Prez **Bill Clinton** will divorce **Hillary**—very publicly! He'll want to marry his one true love who for now shall remain nameless. Bill's been in love (or lust) with this buxom blonde for quite some time but has withheld her name to spare daughter, **Chelsea**, anymore scandal than she has already endured. Big "magnanimous" Bill will finally come clean and end the mystery.

Larry Hagman, again in the throes of alcoholism, will find religion a solace for his troubled life and will bring him peace in this, "the twilight" of his years. (*Is* that twilight, or just the reflection of the light filtering through the bottom of his wine glass?)

William "Grandpa Trekkie" **Shatner** truly finds his niche in TV commercials as he becomes more famous (or should that be "infamous") for those silly spoofs. This rivals his lifetime claim of being a "serious actor,"now that he's finally found his forte.

Identity theft to become rampant as crooks and badguys learn to defraud the system. Celebrities become prime targets when the "no-goodnicks" attempt to pass themselves off as the stars—*also reaping the benefits of their successes.*

Toby "Spiderman" **McGuire** is now stereotyped, and his chances of returning once more to the screen as a serious actor—blocked! However, he'll eventually escape this humiliating experience when he accepts the role of lithium-besotted creative genius, Toronto-born Glen Gould, whose state of mind Toby most resembles *in appearance*, anyway!

Tim Allen will only be thought of as "the tool guy" from his previous hit series and relegated to a trivia question from the *"what else is new department."*

Julia Roberts to part with current hubby cameraman **Danny Moder**. Her too-long absence from the Hollywood scene will render her partless. She'll find herself panning—and pinning—for film and TV parts.

Duston Hoffman will star in television series! It's the only hope for this aging thespian, as he finds himself suddenly broke because of his super ego!!!

Madonna receives death threats when she goes too far in claiming to be the reincarnate of **Ester** from the **Kabbalah**, of the Old Testament Bible. If she isn't careful, like Ester, she may be reduced to "gleaning in the fields" for her grub.

Rosie O'Donnel becomes a guru in a lesbian commune, once again opening herself up to the kind of threats she endured a decade ago which caused her relationships to suffer. She seems only to open her mouth to change feet. But this time it'll be different. This time she'll open her mouth to firmly insert *both* feet!

You will find **President Bush** (the younger) involved in a scandal, but unlike Ex-pres Clinton **Mrs. Bush** will not "stand by her man." She'll create an entirely new nomenclature for divorce!—a system of names that no matter how you spell it, will mean "goodbye my lovely"—*money!*

Keith Richards and **Sir Mick** will part ways because the former finds Mr. Jaggers *snobbery not becoming of a Rolling Stone.*

Susan Sarandon and hubby **Tim Robbins** will find themselves on the proverbial, "S—-list" and their once prestigious careers in shambles, when they are viewed as traitors and Quislings and placed on a *new* Hollywood blacklist!

James Gandolfini of "The Sopranos" hit series has become overweight and his friends are now calling him fat-fella instead of good-fella! Serious health problems ahead—even death!

Much publicized misfit **Courtney Love** will fall into a state of disrepair that leaves her fighting for her life. She's on her last downward and fatal spiral into the abyss.... Some people just can't be helped, can't help themselves, and are simply doomed.

Angelina Jole, to be outed as a "Mad woman" in a tell-all expose penned by ex-hubby **Billy Bob Thornton**. His revealing autobiography, depicting the tumultuous relationship she and he had, will leave her "livid" as she physically attacks "Davey

Crockett" at the popular Hollywood restaurant MATTEOS.

Martha Stewart has run outa time, and we don't mean the timer on her stove. Jail will teach her a brand new recipe for life. I still say its a big "to-do" about nothing—people jealous of her success and money. (Really?) (Prephesied Jan, 2004, Calgary Sun)

Surprise!—**Mel Gibson** will be overlooked come Oscar time because of the anti-semetic slant to his movie, "The Passion of the Christ." However, in the immortal words of The Great Liberace, "I'm crying all the way to the bank!"

Former "Friends" star **Matt LeBlanc** will suffer a fiery death while speeding dangerously on one of his motorcycles. Although alcohol will not be a factor, a roadside distraction is involved (Quite possibly a hot babe on the sidewalk that either he couldn't keep his eyes off—or his hands!!)

Antonio Banderas unhappy again (...tsk, tsk). Seems trouble just won't leave this couple alone! His wife finds him yet again having an affair that sends her lickety-split back to the pill bottle. The *real danger* I "sense" is that one of her kids will get his hands on that bottle! This ends the marriage.

Octogenarian **Kirk Douglas**, married 50 years, shows no signs of retiring. Movie parts keep rolling in and he'll "die with his boots on"—literally—while portraying a hoary cowboy.

Elizabeth Taylor, 72, wants to be a mom again! Her role as an adoptive parent will leave her exhausted and certainly with no time for her own role as queen of Hollywood society... so what's the harm if it keeps her young and motivated—plus, its good for the kid, which is the main thing.

Magnum's daughter caught with platinum blondes! **Tom Selleck**'s 15 year old daughter, **Hannah**, will be featured on the world-wide web exposing all in a steamy threesome with "Simple Life" stars **Paris** and **Nicole**!

Country star **Kenny Rogers**' fifth wife worries that recent Rogers' recordings will lead her new-born twins astray. She is "hitting the nail on the head" with this premonition. Not only will Rogers' "hootin' and hollerin'" send the twins (Jordan and

Justin) down the wrong road, they are going to become a "bad to the bone" country duo—to boot! (It's in the stars)!

Hollywood bad boy **Stephen Baldwin** claims that since 9/11 he has rediscovered his faith: "I think God has put me in a position so that I could have a voice with which to speak to a certain culture" His new-found faith will endure rough times (not to mention his wallet) when hellish Muslim extremists confront him! This may cause him to falter and re-think his loud-mouthed declaration of faith....Oh, ye of little faith!

Val Kilmer packing on pounds! If he continues taking on "avoir du pois," the once teen heart-throb, a.k.a. "The Saint" and "Batman," will seriously have to consider the health risks of overeating in order to see another next five years—else he's looking at an early grave!

Mary-Kate Olsen, teen superstar and multi-tycoon, rival to Martha Stewart herself, has death breathing down her neck. A severe case of anorexia mixed with cocaine use suddenly causes he to collapse—potentially ruining twin sister Ashley's career in the process.

The nine known children of late, great **Marlon Brando** are going to have "egg on their face." They know Marlon's empire has wasted away but still believe his Los Angeles home and Tahitian island vacation spot are up for grabs. They will discover that these acquisitions are worthless, leaving Brando's progeny chasing their tails—save one... *one* will be remembered by "The Godfather."

George Clooney, star of "Ocean's 11" and "The Perfect Storm," lands himself in rough waters when unrelenting fans torment him presents George with another headache—a lawsuit!

Hillary Clinton claims a new book, detailing her rise to power, cost her a chance to be **John Kerry**'s VP. However, it was not this book but her reaction to Kerry's suggestion that she lie low for awhile that cost her the coveted Vice-Presidential position. Out of frustration she'll take her anger out on her dog, **Buddy**, which in turn lands her in hot water with animal activists—world-wide—who then place *her* on a short leash. This becomes big news!—involving, even, the world's supreme animal-rights activist, **Bridget Bardot**, France's super-sex kitten of the 1960's.

"Coal-miner's daughter" **Loretta Lynn** claims she's ready to join her deceased husband, Oliver! This comes in a moment of supreme weakness; the aging singer is depressed from her struggle with double pneumonia! Hold tight, Lorretta... you *will* see your husband again, but not before you overcome this last obstacle. It is not yet your time!

Ernest Borgnine, star of "MARTY" and "McHale's Navy," is still working at age 87 and will be still at 97! This charismatic actor has the gift of longevity in his career and in life, and will probably pass the 100 mark.

Matt Groening, creator of "The Simpsons" and "Futurama," will hit the headlines in an unfortunate light when he's convicted of killing his "secret" (allegedly) gay lover, Kevin Spacey! The ending to this torrid affair will shake the gay community to its pink foundations and ruin the success of both of Groening's cartoons

Madonna—pop diva, mother and author of a successful line of children's books—will snap! When the stress of forever being in the public eye mixes with the stress of child rearing, Madonna will swear off children, and in a new book urge all potential mothers to seriously consider abortion! It goes without saying that this new book will not put Madonna in solid with the Catholic Church.

Ben E. King—will receive a "Lifetime Achievement Award" for his many contributions to the world of music, in general, and to the cause of humanity, specially.

Sports

Due to England's defeat in the Euro Cup soccer games, **David Beckham**'s bad performance will affect his reputation as soccer's super- star hunk status, leaving his professional and personal life in ruin.

Golfing genius **Tiger Woods** will finance a world-wide chain of martial arts schools called "Eye of the Tiger" which *will* flourish. He, too, will become a top martial artist, if he isn't, already.

Los Angeles Dodgers to win baseball's World Series.

Toronto Maple Leafs bring home Stanley (Cup).

New Jersey Nets to win championship league pennant.

Baseball great **Pete Rose** will redeem himself from infamy through charitable works and personal acts of humanitarianism, which'll overshadow his present reputation as an inveterate gambler who is capable of doing "anything for a buck." His face is finally removed from the "wall of shame" and moved to where it truly belongs, in "Baseball's Hall of Fame."

Martin St. Louis, of The Tampa Bay Lightning, is happy now because his team won the Stanley Cup. But celebration is short lived when hidden injuries from the 2004 playoffs catch up with him and render dubious his future hockey plans.

Greece, victorious in Euro Cup 2004, comes near the ultimate prize of "World Cup 2006," but falters when England takes the chalice, ironically in a kick-off goal, leaving them with silver.

T-o-o bad, **Maple Leaf** fans. The frequently defeated **Ottawa Senators** will have their revenge by taking "Sir Stanley" (Cup) away from them in 2007!

HANDS OF DESTINY
Anthony Carr
reads the palms of
Hollywood celebrities

*Actors generally live their lives on stage and film, therefore, many of the "scenes" I have described herein, regarding their futures, will be reflected in the work they do in upcoming roles offered them, as opposed to real life, since the machinations at work in the Cosmos—and in our own Psyches—seem to be the same Electrical pulsations utilized in movie-making, television and radio broadcasts, and in keeping our hearts beating and our brain synapses synapsing....*Anthony Carrr

MichaelDouglas

This hand's most salient point is the long, sloping, incisively cut Headline extending right across the palm to terminate on the percussion (chopping edge of the hand). This speaks of a highly evolved intellect, combined with a modicum of original creativity based on his environment, and not drawn from the Cosmos, through which he develops his characters. (His father, Kirk, legendary movie super-star of the "Golden Era of Hollywood"—1940s—has exactly the same Headline.) There are no breaks or small islanded formations in the Headline, so the thinking process is not inhibited in any way, other than by sex, when it rears it's ugly head.

The superstar's palm clearly reveals that his "Basic Instinct" is to be a great lover (high Venus Mount) and "a legend in his own mind." But Michael's "short" Heartline (terminating beneath his Saturn, or second, finger of discipline) tells us he is selfish in the sack, while the well-padded lower Mount of Mars (that bit of loose skin just where the thumb joins the hand right above the Mount of Venus—and which suggests fighting courage) also causes problems because of a manifest insecurity about his machismo. It is this jealous possessiveness that will bring about his downfall in the romance and marriage department.

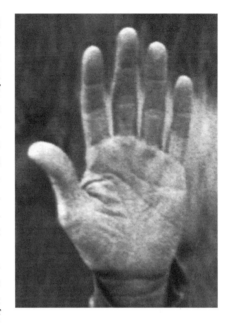

His movie career will remain in the stratosphere but he'll suffer a massive blow to his ego, his sense of *himself*, that will alter his life forever. Michael is a proud man, as exhibited by that superior intellect. By the way, note where his Headline *begins*: it appears as though the Jupiter finger, or first finger of pride and leadership, is *pulling the Headline up towards itself*, exacerbating his sense of pride and need to control. Also the strong-Willed, well-developed thumb and wide space *between the beginning* of the Head- and Lifelines add to his sense of superiority, that he can "rise above it all!" Even his Jupiter finger, being more or less equal in length to his third finger of Apollo, indicates self-confidence. (A *shorter* first finger than the Apollo, or third finger, indicates feelings of inferiority, while a *longer* first finger than the third indicates feelings of superiority.)

People of this hand-type tend to rely too much on their intellect instead of their instincts, and this gets them into trouble. Michael Douglas' troubles will always be due to sex, or lack of thereto, and children.

Speaking of children and family, I see much trouble in the many cobweb-like "tracers" emanating outward—like a fan— from the Mount of Venus and cutting across all the major vertical lines of the hand, indicating innumerable family problems that hinder career moves. —But this he will overcome, because, although these arachnoid-like lines cut across *all* the major vertical lines, these same lines continue their uninterrupted journey straight up the palm to end in a star-burst formation right beneath each finger—promising renown, wealth and happiness—late in life, in exchange for furthering humanitarian causes, such as "Save the Children of the World." (We would hope.)

Again speaking of children, old Michael there, will have several more—two of which are boys. And finally, please note that the "Bump of Rhythm" (where the lower thumb joint attaches to the hand) is extremely prominent and indicates an impeccable "sense of timing," from something as basic as dancing and music, to making important business decisions.... Maybe he'll open a string of dance studios and become the next Arthur Murray. (His father Kirk Douglas, movie superstar of Hollywood's "Golden Era," has a similar hand.

Peter Falk

Peter Falk has a square, broad hand with short, knotted fingers (both the top and the middle joints) which belongs to the perfectionist. Although short fingers—particularly *smooth* short fingers—traditionally are coupled with people of impulsive temperaments (short fingers "see" the overall picture while long ones tend to get lost in the minutiae), when they are heavily knotted, as are the digits of Mr. Falk, the thought processes are slowed down considerably; 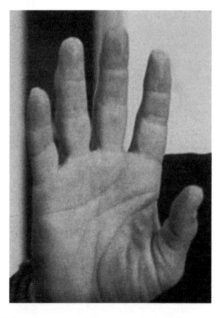 it's as though the rapidity of the Electrical Energy entering the body through the fingertips is slowed by the knots and has to struggle to make its way through and around these obstructions before entering the cerebral cortex.

Therefore, even though Falk is a "quick-study the quickness

of mind to assess things, such as character and script—that speed is somewhat mitigated by those knots, thereby allowing him to rapidly—but thoroughly—mull over material before allowing it to spill out into the world, as it were.

Mr. Falk's strong, broad palm also allows generous supplies of emotional stability and the ability to do any kind of research and legwork himself for any and all kinds of jobs and projects; because, you see, generally speaking short-fingered people (such as he) prefer to leave the business of organizing dull, monotonous work to their long-fingered brethren, once Mr. Short-fingers describes the overall picture to them.

Mr. "Columbo's" palm also possesses very few lines, more or less only the four main crease lines of the Heart, Head, Life and Fatelines—give or take a couple of minor ones, here and there. The fewer the lines, the better the individual's powers of concentration, whereas a maze of lines criss-crossing the palm every which way makes for nervous confusion and fuzzy thinking, especially with a weak thumb and fluffy Headline. This "frumpy detective" may appear "scattered and confused" outwardly but inwardly his brain is as sharp as a tack, as evinced by the straight, uninterrupted Headline which tells us Falk also picks up his creativity from actual character-types in his environment (e.g., probably some sloppy-looking, eccentric street person with a high I.Q. that he met in his neighborhood and got to know, then used him as a model for his "absent minded" detective).

His Fateline (running up the center of the hand from the heel of the hand, near the rascette) is very near the Lifeline but does not touch it; this shows independence from the family (whatever connotation family means to him) while he was growing up—but yet still maintains some close ties to it, since the Fateline is fairly close to the Lifeline.

There is a long gap in the Fateline from between 24-30, which suggests nothing much—except for a few small parts in Hollywood "B" movies as a two-bit gangster—was happening in his career, due to perhaps a poor marriage or poor health (since a bad marriage can certainly produce bad health). But then at about 30 years of age, a strong influence line, running up from the percussion (outside edge of hand), joins the Fateline just above the Headline and merges with it at about 32 or 33 years, this signals a powerful, positive relationship at that point which enabled him to get his career going full steam, with better roles. Definitely this was some sort of mega-influential partnership.

Years later, as the Fateline breaks up into an oblique stepladder effect *just above* the Heartline (age 45-50) on the Saturn Mount, then leads toward the Jupiter Mount beneath the finger of the same name, the Apollo line—beneath the third finger of *that* same name—also becomes apparent, but later in life (about 45-50) because it, too, begins *above* the Heartline. We then realize that he was due for world success through his *own efforts* (stepladder Fateline beginning above Heartline).

The children lines are faintly seen, running vertically up from the horizontal affection or "marriage" lines, located just beneath the baby finger but above the Heartline *on the percussion part of the hand*. This unfortunately portends that his children, or his children's children, will break his heart... over and over again. ("The worst parents have the best kids, and the best parents have the worst kids.") Too bad, really, because at heart he is a gentle soul (bumps of sensitivity on the pads of each fingertip). Before departing this realm, he will once and for all be acknowledged by his peers for bestowing on the world his gift of entertainment.

Jack Nicholson

This hand is more or less of the talented Earth-type, but with his short fingers tending it toward the pointed-type called Conical, if not the downright Pointy hand-type, to use palmistic jargon.

The individual lives and works through pure intuitive inspiration and does not enjoy mulling things over very long.

I am sure as an actor he enjoys doing scenes on the first take rather than rehearsing them over and over. Jack's fingers are of the claw or talon-type—that is to say, they all curve inward, one towards the other. This portrays someone with keen insight into the mind-sets of others; which means he is quick to size up character—the *real* character of people, off stage and on. These fingers also make him extremely moody; either he is up or down but rarely even-keeled. Shorter first finger than third, of course, creates feelings of inferiority which he hides, and that same first finger, curving in towards the second or Saturn finger, is the hallmark of the insecure but ambitious entity, the "I want and I will succeed in life" personality. The thumb is rather high-set and tells us of a fairly selfish disposition (not too much) which is compounded by the narrow "quadrangle," that space between the Heart and Headlines in the middle of the palm which should be a lot wider to indicate he is at least aware of his environment—the sufferings and successes of others, as well as world events—rather than merely the meander-

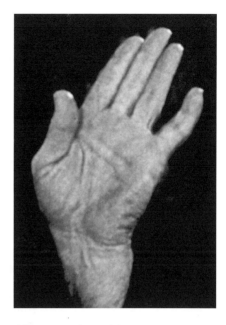

ings of his own solipsistic or self-centered world.

On the plus side his hand is wide rather than narrow, and this mitigates somewhat the mean-spiritness mentioned above; it allows for a somewhat sympathetic feeling for individuals who he believes have suffered as he has "suffered." Therefore I believe this "meanness of spirit" is watered down considerably and may manifest itself in practical jokes while the full Mount of Venus, indicating love of "indulging the senses," also lends itself to doing charitable works, possibly doling out money to struggling actors and writers, which I'm sure he's occasionally done.

The last point and certainly the most interesting aspect of Nicholson's hand is his baby, Mercury or auricular, finger, which stands away from the rest of the digits as though seeking it's own status! And that's exactly what it—or he—is doing: an out-jutting pinky means "I want the rest of the world to stand up and take notice."

Pointy and knotty as his Mercury finger is it does confer intuition, glib speech, eloquence, good judgement in business, cunning to the nth degree, certainly never to be at a loss for words at a party, perspicacity, and, if he were a street person, an excellent pickpocket.

One other thing the baby finger rules:—sex! It stands for the ability to relate to the opposite (or same) sex. And the fact that the tip of Jack's finger tip is twisted means, well... you figure it out... shall we say—kinky?

Jack is and will always be a womanizer, even when the day comes that it's "all in his mind." The Fateline runs strong and true, right up the centre of his palm, meaning his career will always endure, and his Lifeline crosses the palm to the Mount of Moon, indicating the termination of his life near or across water (or as a result of it, such as mixed with scotch), far from his place of birth. There is much writing and publishing in his future, as well as "interesting" sex.

Tom Sellick

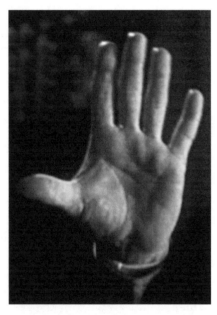

Tom Sellick is of the square hand-type, a powerful muscular one suggesting great health (long, deep, wide-sweeping Lifeline) combined with logic (long, incisively-cut Headline indicating above average I.Q.). This is more the hand of a businessman or a precision mechanic than that of an actor.

Even in his profession, the man approaches the craft as though it was an exact science, like mathematics or engineering, researching each and every aspect of the role (blunt, square practical fingertips) before undertaking it.

The fingers appear stiff and unyielding signaling a similar disposition—meaning, a stiff, stubborn, tactless, blunt, stern, straight-ahead approach to life. Only the thumb-tip bends back somewhat, suggesting an ability to adapt to the vicissitudes of life with ostensibly good humor, which is the persona he displays to the public, that "Aw, shucks, folks," good ol' boy routine behind which he hides. For certain, this is not his true personality.

The Heartline is low beneath the fingers indicating a deep well of emotions; he also posses a powerful libido (large Mount of Venus) which we *hope* is well under the control of a strong thumb-tip. But I wonder if

that too flexible, back-bending thumb-tip is strong enough to control that ultra large Venus Mount, because if it isn't it could unleash itself in bizarre "intimate" relationships, to say the least. A *too flexible* nail-tip weakens an otherwise powerful Will.

We have already seen in the past that his taste in women is, shall we say, ultra-conservative? (Let's face it—they're ugly!) The second or Saturn finger, ruling stability—or lack of thereto—plus seriousness, sternness, depression and even morbidity, is overly developed (meaning too long, too square at the tip, its joints too knotted and an underdeveloped, almost shriveled looking third phalange, where it attaches to the hand). This darker side of his personality—which, of course, he rarely displays to the public (and remember: most great comedians, while on stage, have over-compensated for their almost pathologically—but real—morbid personalities with which they are forced to go through life), will encourage him to lean more and more toward roles that deal with war, death and dying, such as his portrayal of "IKE" (Dwight D. Eisenhower).

Believe it or not, Tom Sellick would make a great mortician because of the hollow formation in the centre of his hand created by surrounding high mounts—Venus, Moon, Upper Mars (on the percussion). You will begin to hear stories of his being involved in businesses dealing with "death and dying" institutes (literally, assisted suicide centers) and burial, whether it be in real life or film.

He may even invest financially in munitions factories, those institutes that contribute so readily to the above industry (strongly developed lower and upper Mounts of Mars). The hollow palm also suggests that although he enjoyed good health throughout young adulthood and middle-life, he will begin to suffer mightily from skeletal problems, particularly in the spine, hips and legs, as the years progress. (Welcome to the club.)

Sellick's Fateline (running up the hand) indicates a major change in career at about 30 years of age (where it crosses the

Headline), probably the Magnum P.I. series; then there is a hiatus, or missing portion in the line (just where it crosses the Heartline), which then starts up again in his late forties and early fifties, no doubt the "IKE" (Eisenhower) TV movie—and promises him good prospects for the future. A budding Clark Gable he never was or could be (too anal retentive), but a fairly competent, journeyman actor he is. Watch for him in forthcoming parts in film and life, which border on the bizarre—even S & M—whips, chains and bondage!

Tom Cruise

Tom Cruise has a strong hand reflecting a healthy, skeletal and muscular system but the finely etched palmistic lines betray a weak, paranoid—not to mention neurotic—disposition and as well, intelligence and sensitivity.

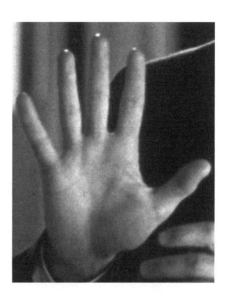

I predicted in the November 1997 issue of the GLOBE that "Tom Cruise will be hit by a new kind of love—like a lightening bolt—and deal with it badly. His religious faith will be shaken when he arrives at a critical emotional crossroads. Although he will never truly leave CHICAGO star Nicole Kidman for very long, there is no doubt big changes must occur in order to bring about some happiness in his personal life...."

Since that prophecy Mr. Cruise certainly has undergone major life-style metamorphoses. He did "divorce" Nicole for another woman,

Penelope Cruz (which, incidentally did not last very long), but is forever running back and forth, to and from his ex-wife's home. Amid huge media coverage concerning his alleged sexual ambiguities, he has had to retain a lawyer to help convince the world he is heterosexual. (And why would anyone doubt that, for goodness sake? "The Oscar Wilde Syndrome?") All these emotional changes are the result of a faint and finely chained Heartline, signaling neurotic instability.

Even though the thinly developed lines in his palm betray an "antsy" personality, Mr. Cruise does have a square-ish palm (organizational skills in business) and a well-proportioned thumb with a nice "Bump of Logic" between the first and second phalange (Will-Power—thumbnail section; second section—logic) with an abundance of self-confidence (longer first Jupiter finger than the third).

Note the powerful Mount of Venus (powerful libido) which is, for the most part, reasonably controlled by the strong thumb. (A powerful Venus Mount with a weak or pusillanimous thumb means the individual has no control whatsoever over his or her baser instincts.) Tom Cruise's hand is of the Mars or Martian-type in shape, which is to say he feels most comfortable in roles with military themes (for instance, The Last Samurai, The Right Stuff, A Few Good Men); however, with such an anemic combination of lines within the palm proper itself, it is doubtful he would ever have the inner strength to deal with real manifest violence in the real world, the way he does in the "reel" world. In other words, the desire and the mental courage are present but the sensitive nervous system will not provide the steely determination to "kill or be killed!" Or put another way: "The spirit is willing but the flesh is weak."

In the future, the owner of this Martian hand will want to play historical military figures: —Napoleon, Caesar, etc.—and produce scripts and books of the same ilk. Many men, like Cruise, have wanted to become soldiers or policemen—but with a strong, muscular hand and an *extremely* nervous disposition they defeat their own purpose. This is the type of kid on the street who everyone picked on and so joined the military or police force thinking it would bring him respect and protection because of the uniform. Wrong!

In fact—it's worse! Civilians expect him to protect and fight for them! Thus, in spite of a muscular hand (and body) the nervous system breaks down and he is either hospitalized or commits suicide. Cruise's hand fits this profile. In future, the actor will experience heart problems (real ones, not the love kind) because of an extremely sensitive Electrical nervous system which, ipso facto, affects the heart. There will be serious—near fatal!—consequences of this, as well as drug problems, in an effort to control the arrhythmia which, of course, defeats the purpose entirely. The accidental ingestion of a "nervous heart drug" (perhaps something like Enderol) will have a near-fatal—if not fatal—result!

Summing up, once Mr. Cruise comes to grips with who and what he is, many of these health problems will clear up, coinciding with the coming inevitable Destined rendezvous with his one true Soul mate. And then peace for Tom Cruise. (Let's hope it's not the "BIG PEACE")

Al Pacino

Al Pacino was born to be Godfather, if not in real life then in the celluloid world. He is tough-minded with an equally tough, hard hand.

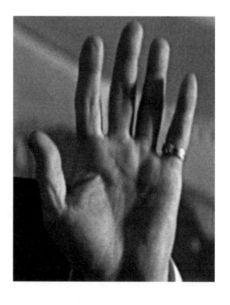

His palm most closely resembles the Fire type, although the pure form is long and narrow with short fingers. However Pacino's digits are somewhat longish so it cannot be classed as a pure type, albeit possessed of many of it's qualities and short comings (respectively: intuitive quick thinking but *useless* at organizing). The consistency of the skin is hard while the hand has a long appearance: you will always find their owners difficult to deal with on a business or personal level.

They are accused by their loved ones of being moody, cold and distant, especially when the thumb and fingers will not yield to any external pressure, namely that of attempting to bend them back by pushing against them. Tough, stubborn and unyielding—qualities, incidentally, one requires to get ahead in the world; on the downside, he also needs to know when to yield—or get broken! But the cold and distant streak, mentioned above, is further made manifest by the Lifeline— that line encircling the fleshy Mount of Venus beneath and beside the thumb—restricting, by it's narrow encroachment on the Venus Mount itself, the natural warmth and flow of that eminence. The line itself should make a wide, sweeping arch around the Venus Mount which in turn enhances the sensuous, warm animal magnetism of the individual and would attract people of both sexes to him.

You can see the Lifeline so restricts the natural flow of Venus here, that the line actually creates an incisive cut through the Mount itself, as though the whole of the Venus Mount was cleaved in two, *halving* its positive qualities. It is, vis-à-vis warmth, emotionally distant. Combined with overall hard and sinewy, slightly knotted fingers, this makes for a shrewd and calculating personality.

The celluloid godfather would have no difficulty making the transition to the real thing if circumstances were different, for he can be ruthless. He has already had a few scrapes with the law, according to the very prominent Jupiter Mount (desire to be the center of attention—plus Jupiter rules "The Law"), coupled with a slightly shorter Jupiter finger than the third (inferiority complex).

Speaking of which: on January 7, 1961, in Rhode Island, age 21, Pacino, along with two others, was arrested for carrying a concealed weapon and spent three days in jail. All three were wearing black masks and gloves and were seen by police "circling their own vehicle most suspiciously...." I guess he was practicing the "method" type of acting for his future role as Don Corleone.

On the other hand (no pun intended—or maybe pun *intended*!), Al keeps his emotional diffidence in balance by playing the witty bon vivant at parties, because even though the Venus Mount is tightly restricted by the Lifeline, the Mount itself is well-developed and therefore still attempts to seduce the good life, as it were, and this act of playing the gadfly and good listener enables Pacino to keep a safe distance between himself and people with real problems, who may force him to make an emotional investment.

With such a hard, bony hand and restricted Venus Mount, Pacino is quite capable of vengeance and zeal bordering on the fanatic. But this also makes him loyal in friendship. Quite a dichotomy.

The very low Mount of the Moon adds to an already moody, morbid obsession with death and dying, which is his stock-in-trade when portraying mobster roles, but it is this area of the hand whence springs his well of creativity—and his deep curiosity about "life's big questions"—death, resurrection, Heaven and Hell... eschatology.

Pacino's most positive quality, at least as a human being, is his long, tapering Mercury finger which rules apt (or otherwise) expression in relationships, sex, speech—including writing and acting. It's longer than average and runs true to an obelisk-like point while the rest of the fingertips are more round-like (thumb excepted) and the top or nail phalange is longest of all three phalanges. This allows him a wide range of speaking talents, "on- and off-stage. Finally, with this type of hand, I believe Pacino will enjoy a long and prosperous career and life, eventually leaning toward the live stage.

I don't believe the characteristics contained in his palm, nor the shape of the hand itself, will ever allow him to be truly "married" or with one mate for very long. He will never attain in the flesh the feminine ideal in his mind. Therefore the older he gets the more reclusive he'll become, choosing instead the solace of his study and his own company. He may even seek out a religious retreat, occasionally.

An interest in politics will develop but he will probably be the power behind the throne. Art in writing, painting and perhaps gardening will become his passions later on and he'll finish out his long life a living legend because of his body of work, much like jazz music great Artie Shaw, who has a similar hand.

John Travolta

The wide-open, short fingers indicate a freedom lovin',' independent individual—especially with that out-jutting baby or Mercury finger which also confers on the GREASE star a child-like enthusiasm. The low-set thumb adds a generous but bohemian quality to his nature. The deep, rich, ruddy coloured

Heartline, along with the heavy, meaty Mount of Venus (although some-what restricted by the Lifeline, but not so severely as is Pacino's) shows a great lust—literally!—for life.

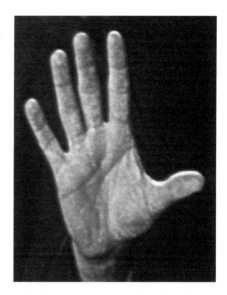

Unfortunately John's love of food will put him in the danger zone. With already suspiciously high blood pressure and choles-terol levels, he'll be forced onto a strict diet and exer-cise regime until he looks as trim as he did while making Saturday Night Fever.

Besides giving up fatty foods and sweets, his ever sagging Venus Mount (to match his belly) clearly indicates he'll even-tually lose interest in sex. Believe it or

not! But not before first getting himself involved in some kind of a libelous scandal due to his penchant for, shall we say, adventurous romps in the sack?

The deep Heartline suggests he feels emotions deeply—his own!—and is easily hurt, but the general flabbiness of the hand suggests a certain insouciance for the feelings of others. The very wide space between the Heart- and Headlines cer-tainly heralds the gadfly, extrovert party-goer who feels exalt-ed as the centre of attention, here pointed out by the long Jupiter finger coupled with a well-developed Jupiter Mount, signaling a heightened sense of confidence, optimism and a general "I-sure-do-like-myself" attitude.

The long nail, or first Jupiter phalange (round tip), gives him his interest in non-fundamental religion, exaggerated by the low-set, non-conformist bohemian thumb. He probably believes (as I do) that God was a kind of space alien star-hop-per. (Apparently this is a Scientology belief!)

The hand of John also warns of serious illness or injury (probably from flying his jet) which he will narrowly recover from, because the Lifeline terminates at about 50-53 years of age and blends into the Fateline, which then in turn *becomes an extended Lifeline* and serves to save and protect him. But this shocking experience will also change the direction of his life—forever. At the same age, thereabouts, he will suffer a severe nervous breakdown due to a severed relationship. Also with that wide space between the Heart- and Headlines, the independent Mercury finger, and especially the low-set thumb, he cannot be owned or possessed by anyone—even if John himself becomes a slave of love!… It's simply not in the cards, in his nature, nor in his hand.

The long sloping Headline belongs to the hopeless roman- tic, whether it be love, life, mysticism or religion. All this is accentuated by the well- developed Moon and Neptune Mounts (both long and low).

He is also an abstract thinker (Mercury finger and good matching Mount), first impressions usually correct (short fin- gers). To this thespian the spiritual world is just as real as the supposed "concrete" one.

Look to his third, or Apollo, finger and you will see that it is nearly as long as the second, or Saturn, finger which makes him one of life's gamblers. He'll take a chance on anything and everything—including risking his life from flying jets, to attempting near-impossible movie stunts. And therein lies another aspect of his downfall, namely taking risks in life and love. (Saturn finger lends caution and discipline; but too long Apollo finger to much optimism—even recklessness!) The long, almost malignantly structured Saturn finger of Travolta and the unusually long (confident) Apollo finger eerily move the actor's mind-set from optimistic gambler's enthusiasm— on into the dangerous realm of recklessness (long Apollo fin- ger) and unconscious suicidal wishes (exaggeratedly long and bony Saturn finger)—and back again, always oscillating. Therefore I must reiterate that there is no end to the talented John Travolta's career opportunities, but I would strongly advise him to curb—just a little—some of his enthusiasm and his morbidity, because even though he presents a happy, posi- tive facade, danger and death lurk beneath. (P.S.—in great danger of losing a limb—hand or foot!)

George Clooney

The ruddy color of Batman George's hand, plus the two very prominent Mars Mounts (upper and lower), indicate a penchant towards violence, as well as "it" towards him. The coloring suggests a powerful heart pumping rich, red blood throughout the body, even to the hands and fingertips. Plus the palm is calloused over and hard looking, signalling a hidden, vicious personality trait evinced only when sorely provoked. Meaning that when he loses his temper

Georgie boy's quite capable of beating someone to death!

As mentioned, he also attracts as much violence to himself as he is capable of dispensing and becomes very irritable and bad-tempered if he doesn't have enough vigorous physical activity for that aggressive, feisty spirit. This high spirit, if not controlled, leads to accidents of all kinds but luckily the thumb is strong enough to keep the Energy in check most of the time! The long Jupiter finger, of course, confers on him a certain vanity and pride which makes it difficult for him to back down from any challenge.

Both prominent Mars Mounts bestow on him great courage and fortitude in the face of adversity, and for this reason Clooney will someday be cited for performing a heroic deed.

His independent Jupiter and Mercury fingers indicate a certain rebellious, eccentric, nonconformist, iconoclastic and unpredictable personality trait about the handsome actor that always makes him interesting to read about and watch because you never know what he's going to do next.

The long nail phalange of the Mercury finger makes him mentally original but extremely superstitious. (He is, after all, Irish.) His main shortcoming, due to the very low Mount of

Moon, is his emotional detachment from—not only friends and associates—but from his own immediate family and loved ones, an emotional paucity bordering on a sense of utter "separateness"; he can turn this "mood switch" off and on, at will. As a matter of fact, he generally shows more affection (be that as it may) to strangers and associates than he does for family members. This will change as he grows older.

Although quick to anger, he can just as easily be quite forgiving (large Jupiter Mount under that same finger). This large Mount also promises great wealth which is accentuated by the Venus Mount's love of creature comforts. There's also a good balance between his aspirations and dreams (Jupiter Mount) and the need to be practical and realistic—with a tendency to underestimate himself (overly developed

Saturn Mount). There's also danger of overdoing drugs, booze and accidents near or on water (badly marked Neptune Mount). He can be stern, cynical, judgmental (Saturn Mount), but highly psychic (Neptune-Moon Mounts). The combined dominant Venus and Mars Mounts say he loves passionately, is easily aroused, but enjoys a good fight with his mate before having sex.

When Clooney is in his dark mood, due to the strong Saturn Mount (strong by its nature means the Saturn Mount is noramally flat but in his case is badly marked with criss-cross lines, much like a game of X's and O's), this creates in George emotional reserve, a sense of loneliness and isolation, sullenness (even as a child he probably enjoyed his own company) and a belief that he must pursue solitary activities for his own well-being.

Generally speaking, George is an entity who is violent and accident prone, who enjoys sports, fast machines (cars, motorcycles)—and even faster women! If he's not careful, I see for him a fatal denouement through blows to the head—possibly shot!—or from boating or car accidents....

He'll be hit on the left side of the skull, landing in hospital or the morgue. But the combination of fine lines forming a triangle on his Jupiter Mount (Jupiter represents luck!) indicates he'll escape death through pure serendipity, experience a spiritual awakening and then play a famous religious figure on screen. George Clooney will donate millions to various charities —including orphanages for Peruvian bastards, but then again, all this might only be a plot from a future movie.

Barbra Streisand

Possessing an air hand-type (square palm, long fingers), Barbra has a massive need to control people, as indicated by the *gold ring* on her *very long Jupiter finger*. It's been said she is very difficult to work with and the above two points explain why. With Babs it's "My way or the highway!"

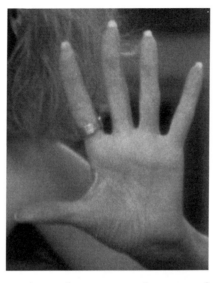

The diva has a moderately developed Venus Mount, which is, like some of the other celebrity palms, somewhat restricted in its potential for warm, glowing animal magnetism because of the *frayed* Lifeline wrapped too closely around that Mount, thereby cutting off the *heat*, as it were. Frayed lines—particularly the Lifeline—are like frayed electrical wires—and means a breakdown of the viscera (internal organs) due to sudden wild surges of Energy output, that are not properly channeled because the fraying disallows proper flow of the current. When she grows angry or when a song or dramatic scene requires Electrical output, her nervous system is severely tested.

The early years of vitality, indicated by the *beginning* of the Lifeline (beneath the Headline, under the Jupiter Mount, just above the thumb where it joins the hand), tells of a difficult childhood fraught with family, health and even financial problems—especially problems with the father-figure—or lack there of because perhaps he was absent.

Despite this lack of affection from the family as a child, which affected her nervous system and therefore her health, the Lifeline does grow stronger and healthier looking as it continues down and around the Mount of Venus. She *is* as intense as her hand indicates and has become fiercely proud, vain and aggressive (at least outwardly), which is a self-defensive mechanism that kicks in whenever her pride is challenged; that *very* long Jupiter Finger with ring on it to enforce pride—plus, high

Mount of Jupiter; and of course these Jupitarian qualities make her a born leader, especially as all three fingers (save the Mercury) lean forward over the thumb; she is definitely a *take charge* kind of person. The thumb, in keeping with her intense personality, is long and strong and held at a 90 degree angle— actually, even wider than that—and signals a somewhat generous bohemian-type. (Although this type is usually most generous when giving away someone *else's* money!)

Thus far we have someone with a strong, intense business hand (square palm) who doesn't like to be rushed into making decisions (long fingers) and who is determined to complete anything she starts (long, strong thumb) and can be emotionally distant when necessary to complete the job (Venus Mount not-to-prominent and restricted by the Lifeline being "too tight and too close to the Mount"). This is a patient and persevering person who will succeed at whatever she chooses to put her hand to. (For sooth—no pun intended here either!)

Although she can be unusually stubborn (unyielding thumb and stiff fingers that don't bend back under pressure) there is unfortunately a certain lack of moral fiber (or passive courage, if you so choose), the sort of quiet, calm courage that sustains an individual through crises and allows him to "stand to" and stand up to a bully without flinching; this lack is due to a virtually non-existent Upper Mount of Mars on the percussion (outer edge of the hand, more or less between the Head- and Heartlines). As you can see this area is as straight as a ruler, entirely lacking the bulge of the Mars Mount. This causes her to not only "hide-out" during an emergency or threat (remember when she thought terrorists were after her and built a bomb-proof house to hole-up-in, instead of seeking them out and killing them first?), but will stimulate her sexually because of the high intensity of her nervous system (note: maze of fine-mesh lines as well as the four main "frayed" ones—Heart-, Life-, Head- and Fatelines).

There is no doubt (at least in my mind) that when she re-re-made "A Star is Born" (first produced in 1937 with Frederic March and Janet Gayner; then again in 1955, with Judy Garland and James Mason; and finally in 1976 with Kris Kristofferson), I'm fairly certain there was some "hanky-panky" going on; what with that highly charged nervous system, as reflected in her hand!

[**P.S. Pssst— Joe: I happen to know that she and Kris were shacked-up together just outside of Toronto in a cabin on Stony Lake, at the home of Rock & Roller "Rompin'" Ronnie Hawkins, Arkansas-transplant to Canada and good friend of former U.S. President Bill Clinton, and who played at his inaugural ball. He is also the originator of "The Band," along with Levon Helm, who played the father in "Coal Miner's Daughter." Plus, I used to play sax for "The Hawk"—Hawkins.]

So *egocentric* and *self-centered* is she because of that *extremely long* Jupiter Finger, that if you looked up both terms in the dictionary—*her picture* would be there instead of the words! Barb is obsessed with thoughts of death and dying—and rightly so! (Long, overly-developed, waisted Saturn Finger and bad Mount—meaning: flat, badly-marked Mount beneath Saturn finger.) This signals danger of death through use of anesthetics! (She is "instinctively afraid of any surgery that requires being "put under." It's as though she has premonitions about it!) And of course the danger is accentuated by the maze of fine lines indicating a seriously sensitive or weak nervous system that could react badly to ethers of any kind. Long, deep red lines survive this sort of thing *much better* because they reflect a *stronger* constitution.

The Lifeline's termination does not cross the hand to end on Luna (or Moon Mount), therefore she will eventually return to the place of her birth to retire and die, New York City, but probably in the country.

The twisted, top phalange of her Saturn digit is a certain indication of nervous stomach disorder—possibly colitis, bad nerves— or both; She looks on the dark side of life (again, too-long, overly-developed Saturn finger) but has an inquiring mind with a deliberate and methodical thinking process (spaces or "chinks" between fingers where they attach to the hand).

Still, someday she *will* make a major contribution to the world, at large, especially Israel—children, gay rights activists— all will benefit (long Mercury finger designed to communicate)—and she will tour the world lecturing on this, her new philosophy of life. She is a non-stop talker with that exceedingly long Mercury finger—and so perhaps politics will be her next career because she's far from through with the public. She lives for it, and will reappear but in a new and different capacity.

Ms. Streisand has a fairly straight-across the hand Headline with a very slight curve at the end, so her contributions to the world will be more of a practical nature with a *small* creative aspect to them, rather than some Cosmically inspired ideology—contributing to education, theatre arts, animal protection, and so on. Later, when she emerges once more into the world, politics will definitely play a large part in her life.

One warning! Because of a long gap near the bottom of the Lifeline, when in New York she must exercise great care in choosing who drives her ("Driving Ms. Streisand?"), for I see a serious vehicular accident after which requires months of physiotherapy to set aright. Babs will spring back bigger, better and so soulful in voice as to bring tears to your eyes.

Charlize Theron

Soft and malleable, like the lady herself, the hand possesses a sense of beauty, balance, symmetry and proportion. Its posture and carriage imply good taste and diplomacy combined with style and grace. Just look at it: a feeling that this belongs to a lady, or at least a nice person.

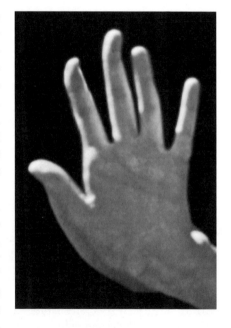

The curvaceous palm speaks of an owner who knows "you can catch more flies with honey than you can with vinegar." This soft hand, with it's excellent Mount of Venus and nicely tapering finger-tips, bespeaks of one who prefers to champion—whenever possible—lost causes, usually taking the side of the underdog (and, incidentally, she is an inveterate dog lover).

The most striking aspect of the hand is the severely twisted, bent-out-of-shape, top Saturn phalange which *surely* must indicate terrible digestion, colon and problems in general with the nervous system... very bad nerves! Because it is the "tip of Saturn" (Saturn ruling the skeletal system), it signals that throughout life she must take care not to break anymore bones than necessary (— "necessary" means a previous knee injury destroyed a promising ballet career).

The flexible hand, thumb and fingers (she can bend her fingers an pollex completely back and down to touch her wrist) signposts a highly developed intellect, a mind that absorbs information easily.

Charlize always *desires* to do the "right thing," but with such a soft hand consistency and the complete absence of a Lower Mars Mount, sometimes "doing the right thing" can be difficult—especially when physical violence is threatened, because that kind of courage is lacking. (Probably in most of us!) She has strong opinions—yes (good Upper Mars Mount indicating passive strength) but when it comes to a "fist fight" the threat of violence would probably deter her (with that weak Lower Mars Mount). She is however attracted to people who are feisty (people with strong Lower Mars Mounts and hard, blood-red hands), in order to compensate.

But it is that overly-developed and lo-o-o-o-ng Saturn finger that ultimately catches our attention: it gives her the discipline and endurance to work hard until she "does it." Of course the length of it also creates self-doubt, morbidity and depression.

The jutting-out Mercury finger tells of her independence, love of freedom and the desire for wide-open spaces while the Mount of Moon, although badly marked, indicates love of the ocean and all sports related therein:—scuba-diving, swimming, water-skiing—but (and there's *always* a "but"), there is danger around these activities so she must exercise great caution. The "X" marking on the Moon Mount itself warns of danger around not only water, but drugs and/or male authority figures born *under* a water sign—Pisces, Cancer or Scorpio—the latter being the worst for her!

Always there will be problems with older men in her life—indeed, she doesn't trust them—but may marry such a "figure" who will one day break not only her heart—but quite possibly her *jaw*! This will end their nuptials not exactly on a happy note.

Underneath the easy-going façade there is deep, psychological damage (extremely waisted-effect of Mercury finger's
third phalange combined, once again, with that twisted, bent-
out-of-shape top Saturn finger nail-tip.

For this young woman there will always be lurking—just
below the surface—the danger of death due to accidental over-
dose of pills, booze or whatever (long, twisted, overly-developed
Saturn tip, badly-marked Moon Mount and Saturn Mount).

Certainly a side to her exists that is rebellious and iconoclastic, even progressive and innovative which makes her *verbally* aggressive (fingers leaning toward Jupiter) but when
push comes to shove and physical fighting threatens, Ms.
Charlize will probably back off (no Lower Mars Mount combined with soft, white hands in general).

Because of her entertainment and speaking skills (long
Mercury finger with its even longer top tip; ditto for Apollo
finger and tip), her ability to… exaggerate?—will one day cat-
apult her onto the world stage, not unlike Shirley Temple-
Black, and she too will marry a powerful personality.

Charlize would make a good "shrink" because she has the
gift of getting others to open up and talk about their feelings…
that Mercury finger and Moon Mount combination gives her
a certain disarming charm—that is, if she can shut-up herself
long enough to listen, because she *loves* to talk—endlessly!!

Getting back to that Moon Mount, and combining it with
a very deep-set Heartline (the first line below the fingers running horizontally across the hand), it suggests that her "home"
and "security" is where her work is and involves a very deep
emotional commitment.

Although very practical in general (straight Headline), the
lady can deceive herself about love—that is, when she *thinks*
she is (Mount of Neptune too close to Mount of Moon)—
meaning, too emotional therefore easily deceived, either by
her significant other or her*self* (self-deception).

As far as career is concerned, once she sets her mind on a
goal or path her dedication and determination is unparalleled
(extremely long and strong thumb and thumb-tip). Her determination can be likened to Aesop's tale of the "Tortoise and
the Hare," in that she eventually gets there.

Summing up, Carlize Theron will soon find herself scrambling for good parts as she realizes she may never—for a while, at least—top her Oscar-winning performance for "MON-STER." She'll spend a few years searching for decent television roles, until again—tragedy strikes ! And once again she pulls herself together to survive by trumping her nemesis and *using* the experience to win even greater acclaim.

Unfortunately I see more blood and violence around her—but it could be just another movie, perhaps about her early life, perhaps a bit of both—fiction and fact, yet to come.

Whichever the case, this woman's life will be punctuated by crisis and tragedy throughout, but *always* surviving if only to follow this, her most difficult path, her Destiny, overcoming frustration and sorrow through acceptance of That Which cannot be changed.

Cameron Diaz

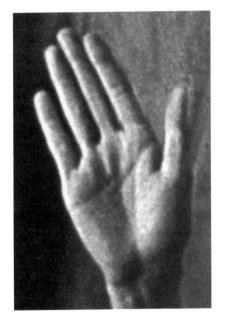

Cameron Diaz and her intellectual Spatulate hand, which means that instead of being heavily-developed around the wrist area where much larger Venus, Moon and Upper Mars Mounts would predominate to create a shape much like an *inverted* pharmacists spatula used to crush drugs (and which area also rules the "baser" instincts), the *upper* portion of her palm, right below the fingers but above the Heartline on the percussion side of the Mercury Mount, is widest (and allegedly rules the "higher" faculties). This person often has trouble making up her mind as to what she really wants out of life. In fact, if you were to ask Ms. Diaz whether or not she has problems making up her mind, she would probably answer:—"Yes and no."

When it comes to love (or lust) this hand-type craves a partner who is strong and domineering; yet when such a partner is found she then resents being put under the proverbial thumb and so then this poor slob, the current "apple of her eye," has to spend his life tip-toeing on eggshells around her in order not to upset the fine balance. A lot of high-maintenance, this prima dona requires.

Owner's of these "higher-minded" hands tend to "act goofy," to say the least. And although Cameron may *act* silly the girl is far from stupid, especially when it comes to making—and keeping—money (long, straight, well-incised Headline with fingers held *very* closely together), indicating an ability to "hold tight" to a buck and a *secret*, at which she is also very good. The "There's Something About Mary" star craves centre stage, no matter how she accomplishes it (excellent long and straight Jupiter finger), and is so meticulous and thorough in her work and health-habits that she drives everyone around her nuts with her nit-picking! (long Mercury finger with the medical stigmata beneath it on the Mercury Mount) and works well with others, even staying—relatively speaking—in the background (Mercury finger *not* out-jutting, *nor* do all the fingers—including Jupiter finger—lean forward out over the hand towards the thumb, (which also rule the "baser" instincts), it's the "I wanna be in charge" placement of the fingers which make for poor work relations (with other people). The owner of an *intellectual* Spatulate hand can be somewhat of an oddball because her thinking usually derives from the *upper realms* of the Cosmos but not so much from good old terra firma; speaking of which, she often wants to save the world and everything in it because of some spatial, idealistic notion that strikes her fancy, now and then, but it does not last long. This certainly is not of the ilk of the previously mentioned lusty, physical *inverted* Spatulate hand-type with its large Venus, Mars and Moon Mounts that revels in sensual and sexual delights—and whose owners, incidentally, make for better humanitarians, in general.

Unfortunately this young actress can be quite selfish, as most young people (and "loftier" Spatulate-handed people) usually are. The *inverted* Spatulate hands, with their greater base development, make them far more humane and sympathetic to their fellow man; whereas the "higher thinkers," such as Diaz, are in a different realm altogether, especially with that underdeveloped Venus and other lower mounts sadly lacking. (Moon Mount excepted, in her case, which appears *elongated* giving the entire bottom portion of the hand a slim, grave or wasting-away appearance instead of a healthy, muscular look, such as has comic actor **Jack Black** who possesses a typically *inverted* Spatulate hand.)

To compound the "selfishness," this Hollywood stunner also possesses a very high-set thumb (which we in the business call the "monkey-thumb") which only exaggerates the "me first and only" syndrome, and if you add one more factor to these two above-mentioned aspects of her hand, that of the narrow Mount of Venus being very restricted by the Lifeline hugging that Mount too closely, we have a pretty "self-centered," selfish individual here. (She refuses to sign autographs for her fans anymore.) To boot, she has a great Lower Mars Mount (beside the thumb and above the Venus Mount) which promotes physical courage combined with a bad temper. Apparently she kicked actor **Liam Carney** in the head and did some damage, being an expert kick-boxer.

She's very superstitious—and probably with good reason! Diaz's hand has the Crois Mystique (Mystic Cross) in the middle of her palm between the Heart-and Headlines in the area know as the "Plain of Mars," as well as the "Ring of Jupiter" encircling the Jupiter Mount under that finger of the same name. So when she "feels" a sense of dread or foreboding, her "instincts" are usually correct! She would do quite well delving into the study of the realm we refer to as the Fourth Dimension, or Electrical Universe. She would make a great psychic!

The Mystic Cross allows her enough "superstitious" latitude to believe that all the women belonging to the previous "Charlie's Angels" alumnae are cursed! **Farrah Fawcett:**—drugs, two complete nervous breakdowns; **Kate Jackson:**—breast cancer, plus she's twice gone under the knife for heart surgery, while **Jaclyn Smith** has failed to find love and motherhood after twenty years of searching—and now… Diaz, Barrymore and Lucy Liu had a near-fatal mishap when one of the vehicles they were riding in went out of control during filming of a chase scene! By the bye, her short fingers also help her intuition, in that she can see the Gestalt or the *whole* of a picture (in *real* life or *reel* life), rather than only its disparate (single) components.

I predict one of these days that her bad temper is going to trigger such a public Donnybrook that it'll probably result in a major lawsuit (badly marked Jupiter Mount which rules the law). Although she'll have many lovers this woman will ultimately be unlucky in love (Heartline terminating on the Saturn Mount *instead* of between Jupiter and Saturn fingers or on Jupiter Mount, where it would normally end.

This marking definitely bespeaks of a libidinous nature, one whose every thought is tinged with "sex, drugs and rock and roll!" (Even though she first has to be stimulated *mentally*, as is the wont of the *intellectual* Spatulate hand, as opposed to the *inverted* Spatulate hand who requires, strictly speaking, *physical* stimulation.)

When seen, this Fateful Heartline also lends suspicion that incest and child-molestation by a relative or neighbor may be a factor in the bizarre or immature behavior of this hand-type.

I predict that Cameron Diaz *will* find happiness and "true love"—for a while (from a line flowing out of the Venus Mount that crosses the palm and cuts through all the major lines on its way to terminate on the Saturn Mount—along with that *bad* Heartline—in a star burst!... He will be a soldier, pilot—some such thing in the military—but will be *killed* in action! Right at the peak of his career—and her happiness!... The grieving widow she becomes, attending all military rituals and services. Regarded a hero, he is laid to rest with honors of which she is proud, but inconsolable. (Or again this could be just a scene from one of her Future but as of yet undisclosed movies. Let's hope.)

However, in the immortal words of the late, great, John Barrymore (Drew's grandfather), who once said: "This theatre is where I truly live, and I don't believe in fouling the nest." I believe the same will be said of Ms. Diaz, in that she will keep her very successful career (with much more to come!) separate from her personal life, no matter how emotionally devastating.

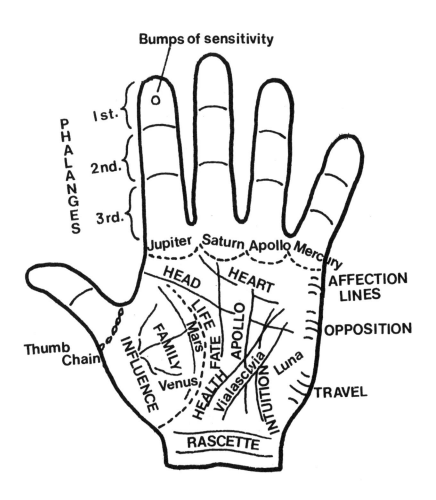

Bumps of sensitivity

LINES & MOUNTS

Was God
A Star Traveler?

The Revelation of Anthony Carr

I remember vividly the dark and windy October night, many years ago when I received the amazing revelation that I am about to relate to you.

I was sitting by the fireside in my home by the lake. Feeling discontented and restless, I took a book from my large library of mystic and occult literature and began to peruse through it. The volume was named Religious Iconography of The Ancient World—it was written by an obscure nineteenth century academic.

I was studying a picture of a religious artifact representing **The Sacred Scarab Beetle**—which was used by the ancient Egyptian priesthood, *when suddenly—without warning, the book flew out of my hands and landed at my feet—upside down!*

I saw immediately from this angle that the picture of the insect was quite different—it actually portrayed very clearly the image of a gigantic spacecraft landing in a blaze of fire and smoke. This revelation was the beginning of my lifelong commitment to the idea that The Star Traveler / Lord of Lords had visited the earth in ancient time and his appearance is revealed in the images of pagan literature, as well as The Bible.

The Scarab Beetle has long been regarded as an ancient Egyptian symbol of myth and magic.

But is it a beetle?

What would a dung beetle have to do with reverence and mysticism? Perhaps it is *not a beetle at all!*

For five thousand years we have been looking at this picture from the wrong angle. Turn it upside down and you will see an amazing image—that of a magnificent **Space Craft** which is landing (or blasting off) in an explosion of light and flames!

Now we can see why this image, when viewed from the **proper perspective**, was held in such reverence and high regard by The Ancients!

The mystical, magical **Scarab Beetle of Egypt** was for thousands of years an object of reverence but people have been looking at it *upside down!*

Not this way...

Photograph of an ancient Egyptian religious artifact which clearly shows the image of the **Sacred Scarab Beetle**.

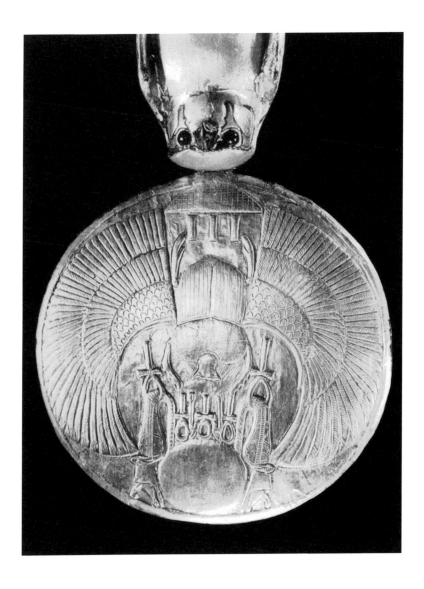

... but this way!

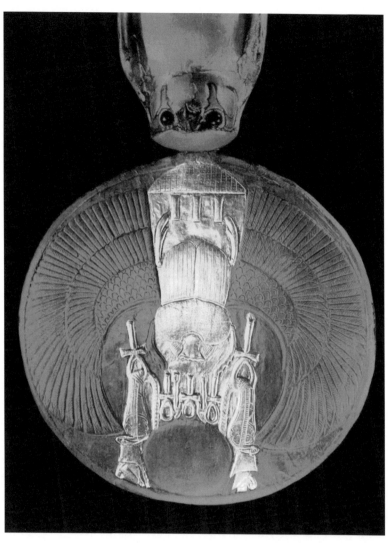

**Can you see
the spaceship?**

Was God a Star Traveler?

A passage from The Bible which describes the landing of a huge spacecraft. God in the form of The Star Traveler helps David defeat his enemies.

From **Psalm 18:**
"In my distress I called upon The Lord for help." ...*David is in trouble. He communicates to his protector who is* **The Star Traveler** *on Mount Sinai.*

"From his temple (the UFO) he heard my voice, and I am saved from my enemies." ...*message received and understood.* "He rode on a cherub, and flew; He came swiftly upon the wings of the wind."

"Then The Earth reeled and rocked; the foundations also of the mountains trembled and quaked because He was angry"... *the powerful engines of the spacecraft cause earthquake-like reverberations throughout the immediate area.*

"Then smoke went up from his nostrils (emissions from the rocket exhausts) and devouring fire from his mouth: glowing coals flamed forth from Him." ... *the heat from the engines burns the grasses, shrubs and kindles stones; it becomes so intense as the engines accelerate, that small rocks in the vicinity of the thrusting, blasting rockets begin to ignite.*

"He smote my enemies with arrows of lightning." ... *laser rays from the UFO's ?*

"The Lord also thundered in the heavens and The Most High uttered his voice at the blast of the breath of thy nostrils." ... *the craft rumbled, roared and accelerated overhead.*

A Question of Fate.
Is our destiny in the hands of the Almighty, or in our own?

The Misfit

Not unlike a writer's lot, a mystic's existence is a lonely, miserable one, because he dwells too much in his mind....

To set the record straight, I am neither a magician nor an illusionist as are Kreskin, Uri Geller, Sigfreid and Roy, Teller and Penn, David Copperfield and John Edwards. They do not deal with things Psychic, per se. Their specialties are prestidigitation, legerdemain (sleight-of-hand). In short—tricks or pseudo magic. What they *do* practice is not to be confused with pure Psychism. (And conversely, that which Psychics sometimes practice shouldn't be confused with pure psychism either!)

It is certain that they do receive the occasional Psychic flash, hunch or gut-feeling during their performances, as indeed we all do, which they will then enfold into their act, but don't be misled: *pretending* to read tomorrow's headlines in a sealed envelope or count change in someone's pocket (someone else's pocket, not your own) is not the manner in which a true clairvoyant functions. Not to take away anything from these very talented people, who are the best in that skill-demanding profession.

Although able to utilize the occasional Psychic impression, even these magicians will admit—or perhaps not—that psychism plays very little in their nightly theatrics—as magical, marvelous and wonderful as these fantastic apparitions may appear to be.

Throughout history the truly great mentalists, illusionists

and escapologists such as Dunninger, Houdini, Blackstone, Arthur Ford, perhaps even the mythical Merlin, accepted that all mammals—including man—possess a special faculty beyond the familiar five which enables them to divine coming Earthly (terrestrial) Events before their occurrences.

In prehistoric times and indeed in existing primitive and so-called civilized cultures, this "sense" was and still is essential to survival. Without it, existence would be impossible.

Therefore do not delude yourself into thinking we are so very far removed from Neanderthal man, or our four-legged mammalian or two-legged primate cousins. Like it or not, we still depend upon our basic instincts for survival. Instincts, hunches—gut-feelings—all are One and The Same, the Same and One.

To pierce the veil, tap the source—the Future—ahh!... Who at one time or another has never agonized over raison d'etre—especially after a personal tragedy, as we ponder the rhyme and reason for it all. Probably in our Heart of Hearts we suspect there is no rhyme or reason for it all—at all. It just is!

The ability to prophesy can be likened to a double-edged sword. It cuts both ways. If this dubious gift is a blessing then it is also a curse. It creates ambivalence, like a terrible accident that one witnesses; too horrible to look at, yet too fascinating to turn away from.

Can we perceive the Future?

More specifically, let's ask for a proper definition of the Future. We are, of course, for the moment talking about Events here on Earth. Good old Terra Firma. Not (for the time being) the Future of any other heavenly body anywhere else in the Universe. Not for instance Mars, Jupiter or Pluto, just here, on Earth. Get it?

So, lets see now... here on Earth, yesterday was once tomorrow and today will soon be yesterday. (So far, so good.) Therefore in reality Earth's Future (as distinguished from "out there in space time" Future), as well as everybody and everything on Earth, is nothing more than a whole lot of Earth todays strung together leading into Eternity. (Or into the Future!)

To the Eye of the Universe, if the Earth spins fast enough all the "todays," "tomorrows" and "Events" flow into one, great, simultaneous Event and Day. Imagine watching the entire 24 hour life cycle of a firefly—and all human life—from a point far out in Space. The span of human life and that of the firefly is no more significant to the Universal Eye than our observation of the cyclic existence of an anthill colony is to us. (Unless you're kinky for ants!) This theory also applies upwardly and outwardly—to every planet, sun, star, solar system, galaxy, Universe and parallel Universe (or Universi)—all can be crushed into a nano second or less!

This may be closer to the truth than one might imagine. This also marks the starting point in my attempt to explain the working machinations of all facets of the "sixth sense," also referred to as clairvoyance or psychism. If only I can put down on paper the information delivered to me from the "Great Beyond" via my Psychic antenna, then perhaps we may better understand this other dimension. But alas, every discovery has its price. Gone will be the magic and the mystery, the titillating eeriness that sends shivers down our spines.

Accepting theoretical psychism is one thing, proving it factually, how it works and why it works, is like trying to nail jelly to the wall. In short, attempting to demonstrate this "extra" sense is the bugaboo. It's akin to trying to prove the existence of God (whether It, He or She be a Star-Traveler or the Universal God that is Nature, or a bit of both).

Testing a "sensitive" or clairvoyant in a controlled atmosphere (laboratory) is often attempted but usually proves unreliable due to the subject's suddenly finding himself in a stress-creating situation. That is to say, a sterile setting with a group of academics at best and at worse several anti-Psychics who wouldn't admit to an accurate clairvoyant prediction if they tripped over one. Most of these scoffers are too pathologically religious or simply just too afraid of the truth to ever want to "stretch," to "see," to "hear," beyond their physical parameters— beyond the finite! I respect an honest skeptic but loath a bigot. Worse, a jealous bigot. His denial is usually attributable to an emotionally vested interest (Christianity, Islam, Judaism), as our belief system about the Psychic Universe is to us.

This kind of clinical or "Tribunal at Nuremburg" adjudication can be unnerving. Psychic Energy is fickle at best. Several theories about clairvoyance and its workings have been offered, usually by idiots. Although most are write-offs, being too convoluted or too simple:—"It's a gift from God"—to actually make any sense, the occasional hypothesis is quite brilliant. Intriguing, even.

People who take a passing interest in the subject have deemed the sixth sense as something Ethereal, Spiritual, Godly and therefore beyond our comprehension. Nonsense!

Psychism or precognition is as much an integral part of our senses as the other five; as tangible (or intangible) and about as easy to explain as the mechanics of thought, sight, smell, touch and taste. The key to understanding Psychism lies in the study of the laws of physics; it's merely another physics conundrum.

We know more or less which part of the brain controls the five senses and even how they work. This we accept without question. However we are at a loss to explain why it works and what exactly it is that animates not only the senses, but life, all life—everywhere!

The part of the brain that purportedly controls the Psyche is the pineal gland. Even though the medical profession still has not determined that particular gland's exact biological function, they generally agree that this one facet of the organ may be true....

The unabridged Merriam Webster Dictionary defines this cranial organ as thus: "...of, relating to, or being a small usually conical appendage of the brain of all vertebrates with a cranium, that is variously postulated to be a vestigial third eye, an endocrine organ, or 'the seat of the Soul.'"

I agree with this interpretation but only in part, because it is my contention (and always has been) that the *entire* neurological or Electrical system comes into play—especially in the moments leading up to our physical death—and interacts with the Cosmos, Which is the source of all animate and inanimate life, not only here, but *throughout* all Creation in the Universe. Do they not use Electricity to kick-start inert hearts? And electrocardiograms and electroencephalograms to record Electrical activity of the heart and brain?

To choose or not to choose— that is the question.

Presently two schools of thought exist concerning *time, space, distance* and clairvoyance or, in other words, previews of *coming* Earthly Events. But remember: we are talking about Future Events *only here on Earth!* Nowhere else in the Universe or Universi because there is another facet of "time" to be discussed later. When referring to the Future (Earth Future) we usually think—if we ever think about it at all—only in terms of this here planet of ours called Earth. But henceforth when you think of the word "Future," please allow your mind to wander beyond these earthly parameters to include the Great, Yawning Universe in which this speck of dust called Earth precariously sits.

So now, let us examine the first school of thought: **"That everything already exists. Tomorrow's adventures are as fixed and immutable as aging and dying. There is no such thing as free will or self motivation or even blinding inspiration that comes to us *separately* from the Electrical Cosmos, or so implies the first school of thought.** (Sometimes alluded to as Determinism, Fate, etc.).

An inspiration, like a lightning bolt, flashes through our entire neurological or Electrical system, *which can be likened to a storage battery, but does not originate in us!* It exists exogenously (*outside* the organism) but it is the synapses (Electrical activity from one brain cell to another) that are simultaneously suffused throughout our Electrical pathways and triggers neurons which in turn allow the receptors in the brain to "receive" an occasional flash of genius. Yet we ignorantly—and arrogantly—continue to take credit for ideas that "strike us out of the blue," as though *we* ourselves *willed* these brainstorms. At the death of the corporeal brain and body, I assert that the Energy which serviced them continues on, containing in that small Divine spark every single image, sound and all knowledge we have ever gained in a lifetime, like a computer chip, which may explain the phenomenon of child prodigies, for those who may embrace reincarnation. (Think memory banks—visually and audibly—of your computer).

If indeed it were true that we as humans could generate our

own Life-Force and ideas endogenously, meaning from *within* the organism, why then can we not create an original idea whenever one is desperately needed. (Such as right now, at this very moment, when I desperately need one to finish off this essay?) If we are so terrific, as we seem to believe, and are in complete control of our Destinies, why then do we not have absolutely everything in life that we want—whenever we want it... pray tell?

This first school of thought may suggest that Man is an Electrical creature, a receiver/transmitter of Universal proportions, whose Energy is uninhibited by temporal and spatial bounds and therefore is subject to the vagaries of Destiny, Cosmos, Fate, Electricity—whatever. It may further suggest that we are not even allowed the choice of which toothpaste to use or when to shower or bathe; *everything has been Predetermined.* If this sounds ridiculous then consider the driver of a car at the proverbial fork in the road: He decides—or at least he thinks he decides—to turn left instead of right and gets flattened by a truck.

The "choice" of direction was as simple—or as ridiculous— as putting on your left shoe first, or vice versa. At any rate, so goes the first theory: that everything that already exists was Predetermined. There is no such thing as free will....

It is, of course, an agnostic argument, one difficult to prove today, but perhaps "tomorrow?" (Incidently, I like this theory).

I have yet to hold in my Mind's eye an image that has not come to pass in every eerie detail. In short, the first theory states that the Future is not a possibility but a reality which already exists, even as Events on this Earth—including Earth itself—are waiting to be interminably maneuvered into position by the Universal Cosmological Time Clock (not Earth's time clock), so that these Events can be played out as they were meant to be. To fulfill their Destiny in Cosmic Time. This is Destiny.

The second hypothesis provides a conditional Future that is dependent on what occurs, or what one does "today." (That is, Earth's "today.") In other words, the Future does not really exist yet; it is there, an amorphous thing, waiting for us to shape it. This theory, of course, postulates the existence of absolute free will.

"I will do with my life exactly as I choose," a young psychology student—a behaviorist—once told me. "Good luck," I replied, tongue-in-cheek. Many years later he admitted to me the error of his ways. He learned life's lessons, as we all must, the hard way. Experience... always the best teacher.

No one can change Destiny, the human personality nor the Psyche and for certain no one can change the Universal mind. These are One and the Same. Unless that same Universal Mind (probably unconscious even of Itself) orchestrates the change, everything remains constant. Nature, incidentally, is merely another term for the Universal Mind—that great unconscious Universal Power that recognizes—not us, not even Itself, but is God—albeit an indifferent one. This entity is not to be confused with the various Star-Travelers who probably visited us over the eons and Whom (depending upon which culture you belong to), we have come to worship as God, Allah, Jehovah, etc. For they, too, dwell within the great Cosmic Sphere Which is God.

The strange tale told by CBC producer Dale Barnes.

There are many examples bearing out the first hypothesis, that the Future (at least Earth's Future) is indeed fixed. One such story that springs to mind involves CBC producer Dale Barnes, who related this strange tale to Allen Spraggett, famed parapsychologist, columnist (The Unexplained!) and author of 20 books on the paranormal (Arthur Ford, the man who talked with the dead!, Ross Peterson: The Second Edgar Cayce)—et al.

"A friend," began Barnes, "a fellow CBC producer was on assignment in Tokyo. When he was through, a direct flight to Vancouver was to deliver him home. Although he was late arriving at the airport he was in time to see his plane taxi along the runway. It lifted off, quickly gained altitude, slowly banked to the left....

"Suddenly it seemed to suspend—just for a moment—in midair, gave a slight shudder, then plummeted—like a rock—straight down and exploded on impact! Everyone died instantly."

"To say he was shocked would be putting it mildly. But wait!—There's more!... Still disbelieving his eyes, he made for the nearest phone—mumbling something about thanking his lucky stars."

"He immediately called his wife to allay her fears about any news bulletins she might have heard about the crash; that he had been late, had missed it, and how It, Fate, must have intervened to spare him—and so not to worry, because he would be home on the next flight...."

"A few hours later, he boarded the very next aircraft bound for Vancouver. It lifted off, quickly gained altitude, slowly started banking left.... Unbelievably it, too, went into a stall—a tailspin—and crashed in a fiery ball at *exactly* the same spot as the first plane—again killing not only all on board—but nearly all the people on the ground who were still working to clear the previous wreck's debris!"

"My friend was killed along with everybody else."... True story!... Fate? Did he choose his own bizarre ending? Or had his Fate already been written in the stars and in the sands of time, thousands of years before he was even born?

The sad and eerie dream of Abraham Lincoln.

What follows is an even more bizarre tale, about a beloved American historical figure, the16th President of the United States, and his frightening dream about which he related to his wife the following morning. Read on:

...In his exhausted condition Lincoln still wasn't sleeping well, troubled lately by strange and ghostly dreams. One night, in the second week of April, with Mary (his wife) present, his friend Lamon, his secretary Kennedy, and one or two others in the White House, Lincoln started talking about dreams, and Mary commented on how "dreadfuly solemn" he seemed.

"...I had one the other night, which has haunted me ever since," Lincoln said.

"You frighten me!" Mary exclaimed. "What is the matter?"

"Maybe I'd done wrong in even mentioning the dream," Lincoln said, "but somehow the thing has got possession of me."

"What had possession of you?" Mary asked. "What had he dreamed?" she asked, turning in the general direction of Mr. Kennedy.

Lincoln hesitated, then began in a voice sad and serious: "About ten days ago I retired very late. I had been up waiting for important dispatches from the front. I could not have been long in bed when I fell into a slumber, for I was weary. I soon began to dream....

"There seemed to be a death-like stillness about me. Then I heard subdued sobs, as if a number of people were weeping. I left my bed and wandered downstairs.

"There the silence was broken by the same pitiful sobbing, but the mourners were invisible. I went from room to room; no living person was in sight, but the same mournful sounds of distress met me as I passed along. It was light in all the rooms; every object was familiar to me; but where were all the people who were grieving as if their hearts would break? I was puzzled and alarmed. What could be the meaning of all this?

"Determined to find the cause of a state of things so mysterious and shocking, I kept on until I arrived at the East Room, which I entered. There, I met with a sickening surprise. Before me was a catafalque, on which rested a corpse wrapped in funeral vestments. Around it were stationed soldiers who were acting as guards; and there was a throng of people gazing mournfully upon the corpse, whose face was covered, while others wept pitifully.

"Who is dead in the White House? I demanded of one of the soldiers. ' The President,' was his answer; 'he was killed by an assassin!' Then came a loud burst of grief from the room."

As he recounted the dream, Lamon observed Lincoln was *grave, gloomy*, and at times visibly *pale*.

"Well," Lincoln said, "it is only a dream, Mary. Let us say no more about it and try to forget it."...On Wednesday, April 19th, 1865, Lincoln lay in the East Room of the White House, his coffin resting on a flower-covered catafalque, his temple of death. His head lay on a white pillow, a faint smile frozen on his lips, his face pale and distorted in death. The room was hushed and dim, the adjoining rooms festooned in black crepe.

Upstairs, Mary lay in her own room, almost deranged from grief and hysterical weeping, unable to attend the services below.

Suddenly, Mary recalled Lincoln's dream of mournful voices and a dead body in the White House. She cried out miserably: **"His dream was prophetic!"** (Excerpted from "With Malice Toward None," by Stephen B. Oats).

Self-fulfilling prophecy of the second hypothesis? Did he, too, shape his own Destiny by going to the theatre? If this were the case, one could argue that he might have altered his tragic Fate by changing the course of Events of that terrible day. But if he had, who is to say the alternative might not have been his ultimate Destiny, as well?

Again, an agnostic argument. But once more I aver that if an individual could possibly manipulate his life's path, he conceivably should be able to manipulate his environment— including the Universe, because in effect this is what the proponents of free will are stating.

Sheer nonsense. The Power controls us, no doubt. We control nothing. Bearing this in mind, it makes sense that Lincoln's prophetic nightmare of foreboding simply had to come to pass in every eerie detail. In my not so humble opinion we cannot escape our Destinies, our "Appointment In Sumara." My granny, who missed her third-class berth aboard the ill-fated Titanic after she arrived in South Hampton four hours late, told me years later, as she lay dying....

"Our Fate is sealed, written in the stars in Heaven and in the sands of Time, long before we get here and long after we are gone. And when we are gone the Spark, that is the Electrical Soul, can be likened to a shimmering Teardrop slipping *into* a shining sea, slowly drifting irresistibly toward the vast Ocean of Eternal Being and Nothingness, to merge, as One, until the Wheel of Life once again turns round to bring us back again and again, forever and ever, unto Eternity.

Thus I believe in the first hypothesis, not the second, and until something or someone convinces me otherwise, I always shall.

Our Unconscious Minds and the Omnipotent Universe are One and the Same Mind that simultaneously interacts and plays games with Each other, which is to say—with Itself. It has dominion over everything—animal, mineral and vegetable—in short—it has dominion over Itself. (Or conversely, maybe not even over Itself!) It *is* the Master Puppeteer of all our actions, whether we like it or not, or believe it or not.

One single Electrical particle of this Power, which we refer to as our "individual mind," not withstanding sleep or wakefulness, can occasionally wander back and forth across Earth's past, present and Future if the Electrical frequencies are harmonious and because it is part and parcel of the Electrical Whole. Yet *beyond this planet's sphere of influence there is "no time"* as we understand the meaning of the word: only that mighty cauldron and convention of all Times! The Great Uncreate Primordial Sea of Eternal Being.

I'm convinced this "Receptacle of Times" contains an audio-visual record of every act and every event ever committed or experienced by man—including the images and sounds of good old Earth herself harkening back to the beginning of Time. Why, even the Fate of the Universe is Itself probably recorded within It, like photographic images created by a Super Cosmological Camera. Perhaps that is what is meant by the biblical reference to the eventual opening of the "Book of Life," a Cosmic computer-microchip, video and/or audio-cassette, DVD (digital video disc) of everything each of us has ever done. (Heaven forbid!—Literally!!)

I can only wonder whether Future (Earthly) Events actually do *"physically"* exist out there, or merely their shadows, the photographs, as it were, like movies in storage waiting to be retrieved from the Past, Present and Future!

(Incidentally this is a good argument for alleged sightings of ghostly apparitions, especially as they appear dressed in period costumes; after all, if ghosts truly exist they certainly wouldn't be wearing garments but would—or should—appear as no more than a hazy mist).

Personally, my *feelings* are in accord with the "shadows and photography" theory. Therefore a Psychic, a much more "sensitive" Electrical creature, tunes his or her antenna into this plurality of "all times" and retrieves from these "stored" Cosmic Videos, images and sounds—information pertinent to his client. (The "holographic images" theory).

We are Electrical creatures, part and parcel of the Electromagnetic Spectrum *which* permeates and Is the unfathomable Universe animating all life. The more Electrical, or highly strung the individual, the more Psychic he is and better able to lock into the Universal Electromagnetic Spectrum.

But as well, the more Energy pulsating through the "sensitive Psychic" the quicker his corporeal body breaks down, particularly if it isn't very robust to begin with, like an overloaded storage battery resulting—sooner or later—in physical, emotional and psychological attrition.

Laugh clown, laugh.

First the body breaks down, then the Nervous Energy, no longer capable of being contained by its banks, overflows and goes wild, ending in illness or bizarre behavior. Most true mediums are usually ordinary, charming, child-like and even immature folk (myself included), consequently they naively view this harsh old world through rose-colored glasses and for the most part are warm and trusting, in the beginning, until life takes a couple of good swipes at them.

Psychics have a tendency to shun society as they grow older. Slowly, insidiously, a deep mistrust of people begins to develop, bordering on misanthropy, a result of years of derision and frustration. But life goes on. So they develop and foster a Pagliaci complex of "Laugh clown, laugh...."

As the years roll by, the rose-tint wears thin,
From Life's realities he takes on the chin,
And sometimes playing, both husband and wife,
He ministers their needs be he great or a mite,
And listens to stories both day and all night,
No wonder these souls, from all of the strife,
Eventually burn out ... for such is their plight!
(With apologies to poets everywhere).

Not only are they trying to sort out everyone else's problems, but their own as well! These individuals possess great inner strength, but lack the physical constitution of the Philistines to do battle with the world for very long.

In the end, they become frustrated, hurt, bitter, resentful and then, finally, quietly withdraw from the world into a hermit's existence, wrapping their dark cloak of contemplation tightly around them.

Generally speaking, Psychics have very labile nervous systems

that cannot tolerate much stress, hence the alternative appellation for a medium is *"sensitive."* For this reason they are
prone to more illnesses than normal—mostly nervous disor-
ders, stroke and the like. One cannot continually and continu-
ously exude Electromagnetic Energy without blowing a fuse.

(In the 2004 movie, "SUSPECT ZERO," starring Oscar-winning actor—for "GHANDI"—**Ben Kingsley** whose *psychic
character* begs: "—Kill me! I can't stand it anymore—the horrible visions and pictures—in my mind! I'm burnt out and
tired—please! Shoot me! Release me!!")

So-called hypochondriacs, *whose general ills may not always
be imaginary,* undoubtedly possess repressed Psychic Energy,
something analogous to a capped volcano. This leads to another problem, booze and drugs.

Psychics should never drink. No sir-ee! Yet it is these same
ultra-sensitive people who incline toward excessive use of liquor
and drugs because psychics, mystics, artists and the like, tend to
be sicklier and more neurotic than most people because of their
sensitive neurological systems: pills, hard liquor and drugs
become the illusory escape route from their fears, hobgoblins
and ghosts.

Because "sitters" and "readers" (more appellations) depend
on this elusive flow of Psychic or Electrical Energy—which
cannot always be relied upon—for their livelihoods, they are
besieged by even more anxieties piled atop an already overloaded circuit board, compounding their neuroses.

Clairvoyants do not have a union. This oft-times can be
quite disconcerting. Since, as I have already stated, the Psychic
Energy is not always there each time he does a reading—
whether tete-a-tete, over the phone or on television or radio—
he is always on tenterhooks, not knowing what, if anything, is
going to be revealed to him by his Third Eye.

Occasionally clairvoyants lose their powers for no apparent
reason. It may last for days, weeks, even years. Then either they
lose their confidence—or worse, their credibility, as sometimes
happens—and begin to resort to nefarious means to make ends
meet.

Eventually anxiety and guilt (if they possess any conscience
at all) will set in because they *are* true to themselves, in a positive way, which means they earnestly wish to help others; as

opposed to those who are true to themselves in a negative way, which means

they care not one jot what they say or do to their clients, acquiring money being their only motivation. And the latter will include, of course, the shoddy, storefront fortune-telling joints with which we are all familiar: the "Madame Lavenia"-type of reader who tells unfortunate, lonely souls that they are under a curse and that it will cost them mucho dollars (usually everything they've got) to have it removed. (To be fair, there are well-dressed executive-type frauds, as well.)

There is no such thing as a curse. "Que sera, sera," and "What will be, will be" *determined* by the Universe. (Incidentally, *no human being can curse another* unless that being lets himself believe it. Good or bad luck is merely a case of the placement of the planets in The Cosmos at the time of birth. These people are *despicable*, and I call them not fortune-tellers but "un-fortunate" tellers! (The *real* secret to cursing someone is patience; if you wait around long enough bad things happen to everybody at some time in their lives. The trick is to be right there on the spot when it happens, so you can say—"Nyaaa-nya-nya-nyaaa—I told ya so!")

Of course the ideal situation for a medium is one where he doesn't need to take money for his abilities and therefore will not feel obligated to perform on the spot, like a trained seal. In other words, it would help to be independently wealthy.

However, since life is far from ideal, there are no monies provided to support retired Psychics as there are for ex-boxers, actors, etc., and so they don't always operate under the most favorable conditions. It is no wonder that they are always fearful and neurotic.

When the world has passed through this current period of philistine greed, we will then train our Future Psychics and Oracles in the same rigorous manner that we now discipline our crack military and athletic teams (minus steroids) and place them in the positions of respect that they once enjoyed, similar to the Delphic Oracle in ancient Greece. (Are there steroids for Psychics?) I sincerely believe all Psychic readers should be examined and licenced by a review board, just as are police, physicians and taxi drivers.

Every civilization has had its Seers and Mystics whose abilities were highly regarded and revered. A new day is dawning, and soon an ancient respect for the arcane sciences will once again prevail. Remember: **Psychic phenomena is merely the ability to comprehend the laws of physics.** In this case, laws pertaining to human and Cosmic Electrical Energy, Life Force, Soul—or whatever you choose to call the Power that animates all and everything.

How do the interrelated parapsychological properties operate? Remember I suggested that man is an "Electrical" being, as are all living creatures, and as such he is subject to the unpredictable behavior of Electrical Energy—Energy that sends and receives pulsating signals (or telepathic messages) like a radio or television station? This Electrical Power, the Unconscious Mind, is suffused throughout all Creation and Is That Which some have come to regard as the Universe, Universes (Universi)—or the Living Mind of God.

Thought, Consciousness and Unconsciousness *is* our one and *only* source of Power, the Piper to whose tune we all and everything must dance (and pay). Therein lies the answer to the question of transmitting and receiving telepathic or intuitive Energy.

I wish to pause at this point to remind you that we are now *not* talking about "Future" predictions *here on Earth*, which we discussed earlier, remember? If we were, they would then be called clairvoyant visions of *"Future Earthly Events,"* and *only* on Earth. What we are now talking about is telepathy, which is *instantaneous* "present" thought or image transference—immediately!—from one person to another the moment it occurs, as in a child in distress instantly to its mother, whether she be across the room, across the World or the other side of the Cosmos!

Telepathic vibration is no more or less than Universally pervasive Electricity—throughout all, as is musical vibration—literally! To wit: The Toronto Star recently reported (August 29, 2004) a story from a world famous observatory that said it recently discovered a supernova, some trillions and trillions of light-years away (through the Hubble telescope), that emitted a vibratory musical note that is fifty seven octaves below middle C on the piano. So there!

At this point we should give some thought to "Light Speed"

and beyond, which is to ask how fast Electrical Power, Energy or Thought actually does travel without our having to get into questions concerning the mathematics of astrophysics (about which I know absolutely nothing), and instead concentrate on the philosophy of it all. I shall painstakingly, inch by inch, in layman terms (The only terms I know), try to explain how this is not only possible, but quite probable.

Consciousness, Unconsciousness, Thought, Instinct, Universal Power, Energy, or God (pick one, none or all of the above) *are One and the Same*, in my opinion. But also, and this too must be clearly understood, the Universal God should *not* be confused with the God or Gods of the Bible (including the five Mosaic books also known as The Pentateuch), Koran and Hindu Upanishad/Vedic scriptures who, in my opinion, were Star-Travelers! But that's another story. (...Yeah, I know, get out the net—he's goosin' butterflies again!)

But when a *thought or a feeling*—that piece of *the all pervasive Universal Electrical Power*—is transmitted, then that Spark may travel at least as fast as the speed of light (186,000 miles per second), but in all probability much faster! (This is, of course, based merely on our finite human Earth time calculations, primitive "terms and expressions, grunts and noises" we use in a futile attempt to explain things we barely understand.)

Yet if this be true, then it explains *The Enigma of Intuition or Telepathy*—again, which is not about Future Events on Earth but about instantaneous "words"/"thoughts"/ "feelings"— or, put another way, about Electrical transference between two or more people in the same room, at opposite ends of the globe or at even greater distances such as far-off planets, galaxies and plural Universes! And with this last pronouncement we are *now* ready to begin talking about clairvoyance and telepathy in relation to different Time Zones— *not only on Earth* (although that too), but on other planets in other parts of the Cosmos, as well.

For example: If I "think," "feel" or "see" (in my Mind's Eye) that something is wrong with my mother or father, sister, brother, husband, wife, son, daughter, dog, cat, etc.—at the exact moment they are experiencing it too, then *this is telepathy*, which means understanding the "message" the exact moment it occurs no matter where it occurs—anywhere in *this* world or elsewhere in the Universe—but is *not* to be confused with clairvoyant ("far-seeing") flashes, premonitions—or what we refer to as "Future" (here on Earth) Events; and for that matter, should not even be mistaken for retrocognitive readings (something I forgot to mention earlier), which means "images and voice recordings" about people or events *here on Earth*, which are "heard" or "seen" from the *past* and are often mistakenly interpreted as though occurring in the "present" or even "the Future" of our lives, instead of "past" Earth Events and pictures and shadows of people on Earth who *have lived, died and gone on ahead of us*. Actual movie images that are still prevalent and present in *this* realm, and sometimes interpreted as ghosts!

The above theory concerning the illusory sense of Earth time (Past, Present and Future), and the World Events we sometimes "pick up," is inextricably woven throughout the "sixth sense" fabric of All Time(s), and begs another question which entails yet another theory... that along with light-speed there is something which suggests that Thought/Energy can and *does* travel at a speed much, *much* faster than light-speed!

This deals with the now familiar theory of tachyons or quantum waves or particles and means, literally, "things that go very fast"—so fast, in fact, they move *faster* than light-speed itself and can go backwards and forwards in Time, like a movie in reverse. (To belabor a point I tried to make earlier: as in a film, only the "images" and *not the actual "physical" properties*, such as people, can travel back and forth. Because an actual "physical" person or property, zapping between or through the "Fabric of Space," would then be in the *present* of that particular world—Mars, Jupiter, Uranus, etc.—whether that planet *currently* be in the dinosaur or the Nineteenth Century period. In short, only the "images and sounds" recorded in the Electrical Heavens, whether they be living or long dead, can travel through the Great Time Continuum, because they *are* only "sounds and pictures," not living or solid bodies or properties *which cannot.*)

Whether we are debating the Light Speed or Tachyon theory I think "It," in one way or another, explains the workings of intuition and telepathy (instantaneous thought / image projection or travel, reminiscent of the old "Flash Gordon" molecular transporter: "Now you see him, now you don't, now you do").

Hopefully you now have a foggy grasp (a fogginess to match my own) of how *mental* images and messages can, like photographs or words faxed or broadcast overseas, cover vast distances in less time than it takes to blink an eye. Simple isn't it? All this transcends spatial, temporal and physical limits, rendering distance and (Earth) time meaningless. We may *now* cogitate on the workings of mental telepathy and clairvoyance, not only on planet Earth but *everywhere* in the galaxies (*including* Earth), and even physical teleportation ("Beam me up Scotty"), but always in the "Present time" of *that particular planet*, in whatever galaxy.

I predict, in the not too distant (Earth) Future, that physical properties (people or any other solid objects) will be teleported to not only remote parts of *this* globe, but to other celestial bodies—yet, will *always* be in "the present" (relatively speaking) *of that particular world*, in the same fashion that our creators, the Time or Star-Travelers, teleported themselves here thousands of years ago, but in the "then present "of *this world*.

In this manner, I have limited my analysis of Psychic Energy—specifically "intuition" or "telepathy" (which is instant thought/image projection/travel)—to the "present," meaning the *present* of *this* world. I have limited it to that "gut reaction" which lets us know something is going to happen—good or bad—to someone you care about (or don't), in the same room as you, down the hall or across the ocean.

The other part of the Psyche, the part which sees "Future" and "Past" (Earth) Events (and sometimes Events on other planets), may entail the study of the tachyon or wave / particle theory which (and this bears repeating) describes things-that-go-fast!—so fast they may go backward and forward in Time, or actually dissolve *through* the Fabric of Space-Time so quickly that "things" disappear and reappear elsewhere without any passage of time whatsoever, much like "stepping through" the blades of an electric fan spinning at full tilt.

This is called "sympathetic vibration," which means if you were spinning "in sync with the blades of a fan," as an analogy, you would only need step *between* the blades, so to speak, to enter an entirely different dimension—thus, eliminating the necessity of a spaceship travelling across oceans of galaxies and trillions of light-years to get from one place to another. In other words, you simply dissolve from one Galaxy into another instantaneously without any passage of Time—at all! I wonder what the "thought" and "Psychic" speed ratio is to the speed of light?

Whatever the proper appellation for our Psychic and physical Power, whether pure Energy, "Lightning" (see Mary Shelly's Frankenstein) or the "Light of your Soul;" and whether or not you happen to be one of those people who shrug "these things" off as "mere coincidence" or chalk it up to a "too vivid imagination;" or whether or not you are a practising Mystic or merely a dilettante you are, in fact, both **Telepathic** (instant thought transference here on the Earth or anywhere else in the galaxy) and also **Clairvoyant** (able to make Future, *only on Earth*, predictions). Your Energy (whatever It is) travels at light-speed in order to render a Present, Past or Future vision. Believe it! And it may travel even faster (tachyon or quantum wave theory); however, the resulting "mental" or "audible" recording will always appear (or be heard) in the *present* of *whatever world*—be it Earth, where we would naturally refer to it as a "Future Event"—or in the *"present"* time of *any other celestial civilization in the Universe (or Universes)*.

Perhaps the Psyche slips through theoretical "black holes" (imploding rather than exploding stars) that create a gravitational Force so powerful that nothing—not even light—escapes, and then blasts it (the Psyche) out through theoretical "White Holes" (which I imagine work contrary to Black ones) with the explosive Force of a trillion H-Bombs into various dimensions, simultaneously creating "Future (Earth) Events and "present" Events of all other celestial worlds (parallel Universi!). (Think of God playing solitaire, and the cards as tiny pieces of Himself.)

The whole of Creation and un-Creation, and whether or not our own Universe is expanding or contracting—doesn't mean a damn thing in the big picture. We, It—and the whole shebang simply may be rushing towards a monstrous black hole to eventually exit through a comparable white one, thus continuing the cycle of existence, ad infinitum. The Alpha and Omega. Ergo, we are all Immortal in this "One Sense."

The Divine Spark in each of us is *Immortal*, and at the point of death leaves the inert body to return to the Cosmos retaining, I am reasonably certain, not really a human memory, per se, but a dim micro-chip or video-like recorded perception of Events, sounds and voices "housed" in the collective Unconscious Universal library, a kind of "sense" of belonging to a vast Ocean of Energy.

This *is* the Power in us that wanders the Universe and retrieves for us our nightly dreams (the actual photographs) from the Great Beyond and stores them in our own mini-Electrical computer, the "Individual" Mind, forever; for It is at once and for all Time part and parcel of The Great Universal Library, in the same manner that one bank branch is connected to another by a computer (and our Electrically-run brain is a computer) and can check your credit rating (our sins!) at any other branch in the world simply by inputting your Data. This Power, along with the pictures and sounds contained within us, *is* you and *is* what endures after physical death; and I suppose (and perhaps this bears repeating) provides fodder for the reincarnation theory, the Christian Resurrection theory (Star-Travelers raising the dead bones and dust which contain a perfect replica of us in the DNA remains), and the Jehovah Witness faith.

It is a memory micro-chip in the form of an Atom, containing a record of everything you have ever said or done. It is there, somewhere in Space, waiting to be retrieved and reinserted into a new player/machine/body—or whatever; this would explain child prodigies (Mozart, etc).

For instance, dredge up in your Mind's Eye an image of a long-forgotten childhood memory, perhaps of someone you once loved dearly but who is now deceased. You will notice that you no longer require glasses to "see" and "hear," in perfect detail and glorious living color, even holographically, the image and comforting voice of your loved one. (This also applies, unfortunately, to negative and unpleasant memories, as well, i.e., war experiences, murder, etc.). Now, hold that picture or image firmly in your Mind. (Got it?... Good!) Now I ask you, what source or power allows you to do that? It's pretty amazing, if you take the time to actually think about it. To visualize an experience "in your Mind's Eye" that may have occurred decades ago! I mean, you should really think about that! It's as though you booted up your own private computer which stores absolutely everything you have ever done or said. (And I use "absolutely" in its *absolute* sense, meaning the Nth degree.) This will remain with you until the day you *physically* die, after you die and maybe on into the next experience, whatever form and "expression" that experience may take until the "tape" is covered over by another "life experience," with flashbacks, now and then, to fill in the "missing segments "of the previous experience," something perhaps we call deja vu.

Travelling at light-speed or faster, a Star-Traveler suddenly appearing in our world would always be *"physically"* in Earth's "present," but never *physically* in Earth's Past or Future... if you can follow this: the "photographs," the "images" and "sounds" of Earth's Past and/or Future, and even of its peoples—yes; the photographs of—*but never, never the physical entity itself,* whether "object" or "person." *Never!*

Even though the "scientific world" is still at the talking stage about celestial wanderings and travelling Psyches (not Psychics), people and other solid objects will some day be able to travel via the above mentioned "speed-modes," but again the entity will always be *"physically"* (as I keep emphasizing because of the necessity to drive it home) *in the present of whatever world in the Cosmos he happens to find himself, <u>at that particular moment</u>, but never "<u>physically</u>" in the past or Future of that particular world.*

Actual *"physical"* time travelling by Earthlings within *this* world or to any *other* celestial body (as compared to "Psychic" time-travelling) is impossible at this point, but not the *photographic images* taken by The Cosmic Camera (electrons, protons, neutrinos, etc.). These *pictures* of everything and everybody—Past, Present and Future (take note, we are now *back* to talking strictly about Earth time here)—already exists somewhere out there in the Great Beyond, and now and then can be "Psychically" retrieved. Or even occasionally "visually" retrieved with the naked eye and not the "Third Eye." For instance, when tourists visiting ancient castles see ghostly appearances, specters of people dressed in period costume which are merely "former" Earthly Events and pictures of dead people—historical and common place—captured on Cosmic videotape or movie film, then trapped in a Time Warp or a "never-ending, repetitious loop," as the television and movie industry refer to it. Ditto for early television broadcasts of "I love Lucy" and "The Honeymooners." Finely tuned to the proper "Frequency," and using correct "equipment," whether "Psychical or technical, it *can* be done, because those shows, as well, are out there somewhere.

Even though a Star-Traveler visiting Earth could conceivably show us images and photographs of coming (Earth) Events using a Cosmic Camera, so to speak (— and since we are now back to postulating the first hypothesis: that all Events on Earth and elsewhere in the Cosmos are Pre-Destined but may occur "here" a split second "after"—or before—they do someplace else in Creation)—yet that same old *"solid"* or *"physical"* Star-Traveler *himself* will *always* be in the *"here and now,"* in this *"present,"* on Earth, or in the *"present" of some other Celestial place!*

The Bible speaks of "The Book Of Life" wherein all deeds are recorded and "shall be opened on Judgement Day." As a man liveth so are his acts played out here on Earth and in the Celeste, whether he believes he has control over his actions or does not. (Do we have some control over the music we play? I doubt it.) Perhaps these Events are captured in the galactic Book of Life, a Universal storehouse of individual videos. The ancient Book of Enoch states: "Enoch was taken up to Heaven by God and shown seven Heavens and seven worlds, and the Future of *our world*..." or perhaps shown only the "movie trailers" of "coming attractions."

I speak of the Universe's ability to function as a Cosmic Camera, Television or Radio and its power to photograph and record Events, as do the electronic media.

I refer back to the example of sending a photograph through a machine (Fax, for instance), or a television or radio broadcast across the sea, and I believe—no, I "intuit," that *everything* we do in this life is photographed by Nature, which is to say, the Eternal Power, and will be revealed to each and every one of us at some point; either at the instant of our physical death (as in: "I saw my life flash before me!") or at some other designated Cosmic Time.

This theory of the Universal Camera, I'm certain, applies equally to the study, art and science of astrology. If you do not understand the underlying principle of astrology, it is this: The

Cosmic Camera takes a picture of all the planet's positions at the *moment* of your birth (called a natal chart). It is the same analogy as the "I Love Lucy show;" it is that particular photo of the position of *your* planets *"frozen in time and space"* that is floating around somewhere out there—forever, and is eternally connected to your Electrical Self until the day you die—and quite possibly beyond! Then as you continue your journey through this predicament called Life, those same planets (of which a photo was taken of their *original position at the precise moment of your birth*), continue to travel (called transits) through the Heavens to *eventually make contact with that original picture* of themselves, thus triggering *new* Events during this, your current sojourn, in a place called Earth.

The current transiting planets (which means where the planets are in the heavens—*now, today*) make contact with **that Universal photograph of themselves**—the photograph forever attached to you!—and create interminable life adventures for you! Some pleasant, some... not so pleasant! But these create the best learned lessons, for they are the hard learned lessons.

And some people who "hear voices" are generally not always crazy but may be highly intuitive and sensitive, as are some people who "see things!" These "voices and pictures" are carried through the Ether to be "picked-up" by "living individuals" (on Earth) whose nervous systems are so finely-tuned as to be able to "tap" into these "recordings"—either audially or visually or both—of people who "are now" or "once were!" This is a group of people who are innately aware of Universal perturbations.

Incidently, this may explain some causes of schizophrenia. Some people—not all—have nervous systems that are so finely tuned, due to an overflow of Serotonin circulating throughout the brain's labyrinthine pathways (much like the fluid in batteries of old makes of cars), as to make them (the nervous systems) behave much in the way a receiver/transmitter does, causing the individual to "pick up" multifarious voices from the Ether—indeed, from all over Creation—voice recordings from entities both living and dead—and "beyond this world!" It would drive him absolutely mad—literally! It can be likened to a radio with a broken dial, being bombarded by thousands, perhaps even millions, of voices.

Perhaps Psychiatry, instead of whacking him out with drugs, might be better served if it structured a different paradigm, approaching the "disease" by explaining to the patient what exactly it is that is happening to him, thereby allaying what must be to him overwhelming terror! By helping him control this Power, it will benefit not only him—but us all!

Some recent notes by Anthony Carr

Recently the author read an article in a scientific journal whose headlines screamed: **"Archaeologists make startling discovery!"** The story alleges that a member of their group took a three thousand year old Etruscan clay pot, placed the relic on a potter's wheel and began spinning it, which is the way the ancients originally made pottery—by placing a lump of clay on a flat wheel and whirling it around with a foot-and-pedal mechanism while they shaped the mass by hand or stylus (a pointed implement, like a record player's needle, which leaves grooves similar to records).

With great care, the scientist gently nudged a pointed stick against the cylindrical indentations in the ancient jug and— behold! **The ancient vase speaks!** Hear the sounds of antiquity! Strange sounding tongues, the clatter of activity, noises of people—coming and going—haggling in the market place, the thud of animal hooves against soft earth, the braying of donkeys.

As the clay was being shaped by its original creator, his primitive needle-like point against the pot—acting much like today's recording devices—"picked-up" the ambient sounds of its environment, which is what this group of archaeologists were hearing!

Now, if we take this fabulous discovery just one step further—which is, that visual images as well as audio sounds can be picked-up, recorded, then stored in the "Great Recording Studio in the Sky"— well then, there you have it!

The following is from *The Soul of the Universe*, by Dr. Gustaf Stromberg, late astronomer at Mt. Wilson Observatory.

"At death our brain field, which during our life determined the structure and functions of our brain and nervous system, *is not destroyed*.

"Like other living fields it contracts and disappears at death, apparently falling back to the level of its Origin. All our memories are indelibly engraved in this field and after our death, when our Mind is no longer blocked by inert matter (our bodies), we can *probably* recall them all, even those of which we were never consciously aware during our organic life...."

Some psychics say they contact this Etheric Great Heavenly Storehouse (that the ancient Hindus called The Akashic Records) through clairvoyance or out-of-body experience, and thus they receive information about past history or past lives. American Medium Edgar Cayce often said he used Hindu ideas to look into past lives to find reasons for health, personal and marital problems in the current lives of clients. The process is variously described as "tuning into an astral television or radio broadcast." Some say they encounter spirit guides who assist them in locating information.

...And finally, whatever your beliefs or not (that is, if you believe nothing)—believe this: That your Sensorial Self (your Electrical Soul, your True Essence) will forever languish in unimaginable agony at The End of Cosmos, where only Chaos and dark storms rage, if you have committed heinous crimes. (Perhaps an exploding Super-Nova in Space is the equivalent of the Eternal Lake of Fire mentioned in Holy Scripture.) But for the gentle souls whose innocent blood has been spilt, is reserved the Soft, Quiet Light of Heaven at the opposite end of Eternity. Who knows... maybe "somewhere over the rainbow" does exist after all.... Somewhere.

Anthony Carr
(***First concieved and put to paper, 1984.)

Nostradamus

From: *The Complete Prophecies of Nostradamus.* By Henry C. Roberts: First published 1947, last published 1975

Note: Any references to the "new-world" or the "new city" refers to "America," since during most of his prophecies were made circa 1555—shortly after Christopher Columbus discovered the New-World—America!

Anthony Carr

New York twin towers catastrophe!!!
Quatrain 97, p. 211:

"The heaven shall burn at *five* and *forty* degrees. The fire shall come near the great 'new city!' In an *instant* a great flame dispersed shall burst out, When they shall make a trail of the Normans."

Interpretation: "A cataclysmic fire shall engulf the greatest and *'newest'* of the world's big cities." (New York City is *exactly* at *forty-five* degrees latitude!—plus both planes hit the buildings at approximately forty-five degrees latitude!)

Anthony Carr

The attack on New York City
Quatrain 87, p. 37:

"Ennosige, fire of the center of the earth, Shall make an earthquake of the *New City,* Two great rocks (World Trade Centers?) shall long time war against each other, after that, Arethusa shall colour red the fresh river."

Interpretation: "A terrific fire, of the same nature as that at the center of the earth, shall make a shambles of 'New___ City.'" (Arethusa was an everflowing classic spring.)

Anthony Carr

The attack on New York City
Quatrain 190, p. 144:

"Fire shall fall from the skies on the King's palace (World Trade Centers?) When Mar's light shall be eclipsed, Great war shall be for seven months, people shall die by witchcraft, Rouen and Eureux shall not fail the King."

Interpretation: "A seven month's war, of tremendous destructive force such as the world has never seen before shall terrify mankind!"

Anthony Carr

Second attack on America
Quatrain 23, p. 118:

"The Legion in the Maritime Fleet, Calcening greatly, shall burn brimstone and pitch, after a long rest in the *secure place* (America, fifty-seven relatively peaceful years since end of WW II), They shall seek Port Selyn, but fire shall consume them."

Interpretation: "A terrific assault by a great fleet equipped with weapons employing potent chemical agents (Anthrax, etc.) shall attack a country which has long enjoyed peace and security (America). They shall attack the great Port of Les N.Y. but will be *repulsed* (by America) by weapons even *more* terrible!"

Anthony Carr

Attack on America (New York)
Quatrain 72, p. 336:

"In the year 1999 and seven months, From the skies shall come an invasion, a 'war of the worlds,' to raise again the powerful and mighty King of Jacquerie (King of the peasants), Before and after, Mars (war) shall reign at will!"

Interpretation: "I'm certain this refers to the attack on New York and the Pentagon. Although Nostradamus was off by two years, I stated at the time that "This event will occur even though the predicted date has passed." And, we may *yet* face an invasion from another world!…Only time will tell.

Anthony Carr

"A tremendous world revolution is foretold to take place in the year 1999 (2001), with a complete upheaval of existing social orders, preceded by world-wide wars," (followed by an epoch of peace, a Uni-religion and One world leader, who restores and *keeps* the peace.

Anthony Carr

Osama bin Laden, the Antichrist, and the Armageddon predictions

Quotes from: *Nostradamus: Countdown to Apocalypse*, by John Charles de Fontbryne.

"Soiled by murders and abominable crimes, this great enemy of the human race *will be worse than all his predecessors!* By the sword and flame of war he will shed blood *in inhuman fashion!"* (P.421, CX,Q10)

"The Antichrist will soon annihilate three countries. The war he will wage will last twenty-seven years. Opponents will be put to death and prisoners deported. Blood from bodies will redden the water, the land will be riddled with blows (missiles, bombardments)." (P.423, CVIII, Q17)

The airborne invasion of New York

"In july 1999 (september 11, 2001) a great, terrifying leader will *come through the skies* to revive (the memory of) the great conqueror angoulême. Before and after, war will rule luckily." (Cx, 972)

Powerful enemy hidden within bosom of New York City
Quatrain 92, p.308:

"The King shall desire to enter into the 'New City.' With foes they shall come to overcome it, The prisoner being freed, shall speak and act falsely, The King being gotten out, shall keep far from enemies."

Interpretation: "The 'New City' (New York?) shall be besieged by a powerful person, helped by spies within!"   Anthony Carr

A tidal wave of putrid water throughout New York, New Jersey or Atlantic City
Quatrain 49, p. 328:

"Garden of the World (Garden State?), near the New City (New York?), in the way of the *Man-made mountains* (Skyscrapers?), Shall be seized on and plunged into a ferment (putrid), Being forced to drink sulphurous poisoned waters."

Interpretation: "This startling prophecy of a catastrophic event at a pleasure resort not far from the great 'new city,' predicts a tremendous tidal wave of poisoned waters that shall sweep in from 'the resort' and overwhelm the man-made mountain-like skyscrapers of the city."

One religion—for all!
Quatrain 72, p. 302:

"Once more shall the Holy Temple be polluted, And depredated by the Senate of Toulouse, Saturn two, three cycles revolving, In April, May, people of a new heaven."

Interpretation: "According to this prophecy, there will be a complete revision of the basic concepts of religion about the year 2150 (600 years after it was written), and a 'new-world' (America?) Order will arise" (possibly one religion for *all!*).

Terrible war, followed by a 'new-world' leader who will initiate a long peace
Quatrain 24, p. 187:

"Mars and the Secptre, being conjoined together, Under Cancer shall be a calamitous war, A little while after a new King shall be anointed, Who, for a long time, shall pacify the earth."

Interpretation: "Nostradamus here speaks of a constellation called the Sceptre. Looking at what was then the far future (1555), he foretells of a time when this constellation shall be in conjunction with Mars, and the *terrible* war that will break out under this influence. And out of the debacle there will arise a "new-world" leader ("new-world," United States President?) and peace will reign for a long time afterward."

Quatrain 70, p. 202:

"A chief of the world, the great Henry shall be, at first, beloved, afterwards feared, dreaded, His fame and praise shall go beyond the heavens! And shall be contented with the title of Victor."

Interpretation: "The nations will organize a super-government covering the entire world! The president will be called, or named, Henry. "Chryen' by transposition of letters is an anagram for "Henry,' then current form of Henry."

Eventual world peace (egalitarianism)
Quatrain 10, p. 182:

"Within a little while the temples of the colors, White and black shall be *intermixed*, red and yellow shall take away their colors, Blood, earth, plague, famine, fire, water shall destroy them."

Interpretation: "After a period of much travail *all* the races of the world shall lose their prejudices and be as *one*."

Quatrain 89, pg. 341:

"The walls shall be turned from brick into marble, There shall be peace for seven and fifty years, Joy to mankind; the aqueduct shall be rebuilt, Health, abundance of fruits, joys and a mellifluous time."

Interpretation: "Nostradamus predicts a golden age for humanity after a great calamitous war among nations." (Personally, I think this refers to the end of World War II till the present—*exactly* fifty seven years (1945-2002), then hostilities begin anew!)
                                                              Anthony Carr

Yet another prediction of eventual world peace
Quatrain 66, p. 300:

"Peace, union, shall be and profound changes, Estates, offices, the low high and the high very low A journey shall be prepared for, the first fruit, pains, War shall cease, also civil processes and strife."

Interpretation: "A Utopian age shall come into being in the course of time, but not without pain."

Quatrain 96, p. 344:

"Religion of the name of the seas shall come, Against the Sect of 'Caitif of the Moon,' The deplorably obstinate sect, shall be afraid, Of the two wounded by A. and A."

Interpretation: "One must delve deeply into these cryptic words in order to grasp their full meaning. The 'Caitifs of the Moon' indicates the Arab nation. The phrase "A. and A." means America. The sense, then, is that there will be a struggle between the opposing philosophies of the two groups." (To say the *least*—hindsight!)

Now we can see it: "Religion of the name of the seas shall come, against the *'Sect of Caitifs of the Moon'* (Arab Nations flag is the quarter-moon and star; the word 'Caitif' in the Unabridged Oxford Dictionary means: base, cowardly and despicable), the deplorably obstinate sect *shall* be afraid of the two wounded by A. and A. This *sneaky, cowardly murderous* people shall become *afraid* of, then *destroyed* by, A. and A.— America!!!

Anthony Carr

The sudden end of global war!
Quatrain 53, p. 162:

"The law of Sun and Venus contending, appropriating the spirit of prophecy, Neither one nor the other shall be heard, By Sol the law of the great Messiah shall subsist."

Interpretation: "The forces of light and darkness, struggling for domination over the spirit of man, shall *both* be superseded by the new law of the great Saviour!" (Or, if I may suggest, "The Great and Mighty One will halt the carnage, lest *all* flesh perish!…Supreme Star-traveller, or God, who created us *all*— Christian, Muslim and Jew.)

Quatrain 99, p. 345:

"At last the wolf, the lion, ox and ass, The gentle doe, shall be down with mastiffs. The Manna shall no more fall to them, There shall be no more watching and keeping of mastiffs."

Interpretation: "This reiterates previous Prognostications of a period of peace and plenty, and of elimination of *war.*"

And peace!!!
Anthony Carr

Religion

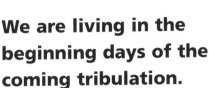

We are living in the beginning days of the coming tribulation.

A mighty sign in the heavens shall apprise us of the Great One's return. (Star-Traveler, Lord of Lords, King of Kings!

From the sky Gods you will hear and know everything. I predict Eternal God shall tread upon the Earth and on that day all shall be smitten with fear and trembling—even unto the ends of the earth!

Terrible upheavals! The high mountains shall be shaken, the high hills made low; (nearly) all that is upon the earth shall perish, and there shall be a Judgment on every man (and woman).

Truly the kind and the righteous. He shall save and protect. But not the hypocrites!

There is soon to be another pandemic Cosmic shock to our collective Psyche, which must occur to modify man's violent behavior, to put back the fear of God in us. And soon!

The Antichrist will rise out of Africa, evil as black as his heart. To the dark place shall shift the turmoil. He tears the world apart. Once, twice, removed from the East!—the sojourn hails his new start. (P.S. We will all recognize him as being from the past.)

But first, behold! He cometh with ten thousand times ten thousand of His holy ones (astronauts), to execute Judgment upon all and to destroy the ungodly!

Then the angels (extraterrestrial astronauts), the children of heaven, will once again lust after the daughters of men, and take unto themselves from among them, wives.

Then shall He make peace with the Elect, and they shall prosper.

But before the Peace, a great destruction shall be wrought upon the earth, and men shall know agony for five months and three days; he shall see the destruction of his children, and all whom he loves, over and over again, but mercy and peace shall he not attain.

Then a great light shall descend from heaven, coming down like a brilliant, many-colored jewel, and the King of Kings shall step forward to save the world, less all perish! (i.e., Commander in Chief of astronauts, head Honcho—etc..)So sparkling will be his raiment that all the inhabitants of the world will not look upon it directly.

Then shall the Great and Glorious One sit upon his earthly throne thereon. And his raiment more bright than the sun and all the stars, shall hold the children of earth in awe, and He shall judge the world.... (from the Ancient Book of Enoch, with commentary by Anthony Carr)

"In God's high place above the world and the firmament, I proceeded to where everything was chaotic and horrible: I saw neither heaven alone nor a firmly founded earth but a place terrible and awful! And it was burning with fire. And I asked the angel (astronaut): 'For what sin are they bound and on what account have they been cast in hither?'

"Then said Uriel, the angel of the Lord, said unto me: 'why dost thou ask, and why art thou eager for the truth? These souls have transgressed the commandment of the Lord and are bound here till ten thousand years, the time allotted for their sins, are consummated'

"And from thence, I went to another place, which was more terrible than the former, and I saw a horrible thing: a great fire there which burnt and blazed!

"Then I said: 'How fearful is this place and how terrible to look upon!' Then Uriel answered me, and said: 'Enoch, why hast though such fear and affright?' And I answered, 'Because of this fearful place, and because of the spectacle of the pain!'

"And he said unto me: 'This place is the prison of the (evil) angels, and here they will be imprisoned forever!' (In this terrible and chaotic corner of the Universe—hell! Yet the good angels—"Souls"—shall bask in the soft light of God's Eternal heaven.)

"Then Uriel said unto me: 'Here their spirits shall be set apart (in heaven and hell) till the great day of Judgment, and the punishment and torment of those who curse forever, and the retribution for their sins, and for even the false Christendom" (the false church).

His Judgment cometh, and that right soon: The cities like unto Sodom and Gomorrah shall be destroyed first, at the outbreak of Armageddon.

"And there, above the earth and the firmament, I came face to face with the King of Heaven, the God of Glory ("Glory" means bright light), and mine eyes saw the secrets of the lightning's, and the lights, and the peels of thunder by which the Lord executed his command."

(Probably aboard a UFO, Enoch was bedazzled and bewildered by the maze of flashing colored lights and booming loudspeakers through which orders were barked. Remember: this is a primitive cave dweller, completely ignorant of electricity-or superior energy power-and all of its multi-faceted uses.)

"I alone have seen this vision, the end of all things, and no man shall see as I have seen." From "The Ancient Book of Enoch"

The beautiful story of Christmas

A modern interpretation, of course, by Anthony Carr.

I have always believed that the star of Bethlehem was a UFO, which led the three Magi to the Christ child. That Mary was put into a deep sleep by the Archangel/Star-Traveler Gabriel and, through some form of extra-terrestrial artificial insemination, impregnated her and—viola!—a superior human being, who was and was not of this world, was conceived (the virgin birth); and the angel of the Lord who appeared to the shepherds "watching over their flocks by night" was most certainly an extraterrestrial astronaut.

A theory that his resurrection could have been the result of the cloning of his own body's DNA, and his "ascension into

heaven," perhaps to the Mother ship and head-Honcho Star-
Traveller, a sort of a "Beam me up, Scotty!" will be proffered
by someone other than me (for a change), a respected member of the scientific community.

Thus we have the beautiful story of Christmas:

"And God (the "good" Star-Traveller) sent the angel Gabriel
(one of his astronauts) to a city of Galilee named Nazareth, to
a virgin named Mary who was betrothed to a man called
Joseph; and the angel appeared to her, and said, 'Hail, O
favored one, the Lord is with you! Do not be afraid, Mary, for
you have found favor with God.'

'And behold, you will conceive in your womb and bear a
son, and you shall call his name Jesus. He will be great, and
will be called the Son of the Most High; and the Lord God will
give to him the throne of his father, David, and of his kingdom
there will be no end; and he will reign over the house of Jacob
forever.'

"And Mary said to the angel, 'How shall this be, since I have
no husband?' And the angel said to her, 'The Holy Spirit will
come upon you (advanced technical type of impregnation)
and the power of the Most High will overshadow you; therefore, the child to be born will be called Holy, the Son of God.'
(Luke 1:26-35)

"And there were shepherds out in the field keeping watch
over their flocks by night. (Again) an angel of the Lord
appeared to them and the glory (very bright lights) of the Lord
shone around them, and they were filled with fear."
(Throughout the Bible whenever 'the glory of the Lord' is
mentioned it always pertains to brightly shining lights which,
centuries before the advent of electricity, certainly would
seem like a 'glorious' miracle, indeed.)

"And the angel said to them, 'Be not afraid; for behold, I
bring you good tidings of great joy which shall be to all men;
for to you is born this day in the city of David a Savior, who is
Christ the Lord. And this will be a sign unto you; you will find
a babe wrapped in swaddling clothes and lying in a manger.'

"And suddenly there was with the angel a multitude of the
heavenly host (many celestial astronauts with either oxygen
tanks or levitating devices on their backs, often depicted in
Christian religion paintings as 'wings'—who were frolicking to

and fro), praising God and saying, 'Glory to God in the highest, and on Earth, peace and goodwill toward men with whom he is pleased.' When the angels went away from them into heaven," etc.... (Luke 2:8-15)

And then there were the three wise men who followed the star of Bethlehem, a very brilliantly lit UFO: "And lo, the star which they had seen in the east went before them (that is, led them, till it came to rest, or stop) over the place where the child was."

The Old and New Testaments are rife with stories about Star-Travelers, e.g., when Moses brought the people of Israel up to Mt. Sinai:

"Thus the Lord used to speak to Moses, face to face, as a man speaks to his friend." (Exodus 33:11)

And as well: Psalm 18 is stronglydescriptive of a UFO (unidentified flying object):

"In my distress I called upon the Lord for help." (David is in trouble, so he communicates with his protector, the Star-Traveler, on Mt. Sinai): "From his temple (the UFO) he heard my voice, and I am saved from my enemies." (Message received and understood.) "Then the earth reeled and rocked; the foundations also of the mountains trembled and quaked because he was angry" (The powerful engines of a rocket or space craft cause earthquake-like reverberations throughout the immediate area.) "Then smoke went up from his nostrils (emissions from the rocket exhausts), and devouring fire from his mouth; glowing coals flamed forth from him." (The heat from the engines burns the grasses, shrubs and kindles stones; it becomes so intense, as the engines accelerate, that small rocks in the vicinity of the thrusting, blasting rockets begin to ignite.) "He smote mine enemies with arrows of lightning. (Laser rays from the UFO's?)

"The Lord also thundered in the heavens, and the Most High uttered his voice at the blast of the breath of thy nostrils." (The craft rumbled, roared and accelerated overhead. It's no wonder David spent so much time singing praises to the Lord, or Star-Traveler, he would have been a dead duck without him.)

The lovely story of Easter:

"Now after the Sabbath, toward the dawn of the first day of the week, Mary Magdalene and the other Mary went to the sepulcher. And behold, there was a great earthquake (hovering space craft causing the ground to tremble?); for an Angel (astronaut) of the Lord (head Honcho Star-Traveler?) descended from heaven and came and rolled back the stone, and sat upon it.

"His appearance was like lighting and his raiment white as snow." (Probably because of his phosphorus-like, or shiny space suit resembling those that the earth astronauts wore during the 1969 moon landing.)

Mathew 8:1-20

Watch the heavens for the return of the Star-Travelers, who will intervene in the affairs of Man and halt the violence: "And I saw the holy city (gloriously brilliant UFO), new Jerusalem, coming down out of the heaven from God, prepared as a bride adomed for her husband; having the glory of God, its radiance like a most rare jewel, a jasper, clear as crystal.

"And I heard a loud voice from the throne saying, "Behold, the dwelling of God is with men. He will dwell with them, and they shall be his people, and God, himself (supreme Star Chief), will be with them;

"He will wipe away every tear from their eyes, and death shall be no more, neither shall there be mourning nor crying nor pain anymore."

Revelation 21:1-4 & 11

Watch! For they are coming! And there shall be peace...

To you, my friend, I wish

A very merry Christmas and a happy New Year!

Anthony Carr